Land Registry fees

The fees reproduced in this section are prescribed by the Land Registration Fees Order 2003, SI 2003/165, which came into force on 1 March 2003.

1.1 Scale 1 (Schedule 1)
First registrations and transfers for monetary consideration

Value or amount (£)	Fee (£)	Reduced fee (£)
0 to 50,000	40	30
50,001 to 80,000	60	45
80,001 to 100,000	100	75
100,001 to 200,000	150	110
200,001 to 500,000	250	190
500,001 to 1,000,000	450	340
1,000,001 and over	750	560

Note 1: Where the amount or value is a figure which includes pence, it may be rounded down to the nearest £1.

Note 2: The reduced fee in column 3 applies to voluntary registrations (see art 2(5)).

Note 3: The fee for an application for first registration of title to a lease by the original lessee or his PR shall be paid in accordance with above scale on an amount calculated as follows:

$A = P + (10 \times R)$ where:

A = the amount on which the fee is to be paid

P = the amount or value of any monetary consideration given by the lessee as part of the transaction by way of premium etc.

R = the largest ascertainable amount of annual rent reserved by the lease (see art 2(3)).

Note 4: Where no monetary consideration is given by the lessee as part of the transaction; and no annual rent is reserved, or the annual rent cannot be ascertained at the date of the application, a fee shall be paid in accordance with Scale 1 on the value of the lease calculated in accordance with art 7, subject to a minimum fee of £40.

1.2 Scale 2 (Schedule 2)
Transfers otherwise than for monetary consideration

Value or amount (£)	Fee (£)
0 to 100,000	40
100,001 to 200,000	50
200,001 to 500,000	70
500,001 to 1,000,000	100
1,000,001 and over	200

Note 1: Where the amount or value is a figure which includes pence, it may be rounded down to the nearest £1.

Note 2: The fee for an application for registration of any of the following transactions shall be paid in accordance with Scale 2 on the value of the land subject to the dealing after deducting the amount secured upon the land by any charge subject to which the registration takes effect. Those transactions are:

- Transfer of registered land otherwise than for monetary consideration
- Surrender of a registered lease otherwise than for monetary consideration
- Transmission of registered land on death or bankruptcy
- Assent of registered land (including a vesting assent)
- Appropriation of registered land
- Vesting order or declaration under s 47 of the Land Registration Act 1925
- Rectification of the register
- Transfer of a matrimonial home (being registered land) made pursuant to order of the court (art 4).

Note 3: Where a transfer gives effect to the disposition of a share in registered land, the fee shall be calculated on the value of that share (art 4(2)).

Note 4: In the case of rectification of the registers, the Registrar may reduce or waive the fee (art 4(3)).

1.3 Schedule 3
Part I: Fixed fee applications

Fee

(1) To register or modify a caution, a restriction (other than a restriction to which paragraph (10) of Schedule 4 applies), a notice, an inhibition, or a note for which no other provision is made by this Order and for which the Registrar considers a fee should be paid:

- total fee for up to three titles — £40
- additional fee for each subsequent title — £20

FEES, DUTIES AND TAXES: 1 LAND REGISTRY FEES

Provided that no such fee shall be payable if, in relation to each registered title affected, the application is accompanied by scale fee application or another application which attracts a fee under this paragraph.

(2) To close or partly close a registered leasehold or rentcharge title other than on surrender (whether or not the surrender is for monetary consideration and whether effected by deed or otherwise) – for each title closed or partly closed. £40

Provided that no such fee shall be payable if the application is accompanied by a scale fee application.

(3) To convert from one class of title to another £40

Provided that no fee shall be payable if the application for conversion is accompanied by a scale fee application.

(4) Application under rule 271 of the principal rules in relation to a lost or destroyed land certificate or charge certificate (in addition to the cost of any advertisement):

    (a) where a replacement certificate is issued £40
    (b) where a replacement certificate is not issued £20

(5) First registration of a title to a rentcharge £40

(6) To cancel an entry in the register of notice of an unregistered rentcharge which has determined on merger, redemption or otherwise – for each title affected £40

Provided that no such fee shall be payable if the application is accompanied by a scale fee application.

(7) An outline application to secure priority for a dealing with registered land which cannot be protected by an official search with priority of the register:

    (a) where delivered by direct access to the Registrar's computer system by means of a person's remote terminal £2
    (b) where delivered by any other means £4

such fee to be payable in addition to any other fee which is payable in respect of the application.

Part II: Services – inspection and copying

    Fee

(1) Inspection of the following, including in each case the making of a copy, on any one occasion when a person gains access to the Registrar's computer system by means of that person's remote terminal pursuant to rule 4A of the Land Registration (Open Register) Rules 1991:

    (a) the register or any part of the register – per title £2
    (b) the title plan – per title £2
    (c) any or all of the documents referred to in the register (other than documents referred to in paragraph (4) below) – per title £2

THE CONVEYANCER'S FACTFINDER

FEES, DUTIES AND TAXES: 1 LAND REGISTRY FEES

(2) Inspection (otherwise than under paragraph (1) above):

(a) of the register or any part thereof – per title	£4
(b) of the title plan – per title	£4
(c) of any or all of the documents referred to in the register (other than documents referred to in paragraph (4) below) – per title	£4

(3) Office copy in respect of a registered title:

(a) of the register of any part thereof – per copy
(i) where requested from a person's remote terminal and permitted in accordance with a notice given pursuant to rule 13 of the Land Registration (Open Register) Rules 1991 — £2
(ii) where requested by any other permitted means — £4
(b) of the title plan – per copy
(i) where requested from a person's remote terminal and permitted in accordance with a notice given pursuant to rule 13 of the Land Registration (Open Register) Rules 1991 — £2
(ii) where requested by any other permitted means — £4
(c) of any or all of the documents referred to in the register (other than documents referred to in paragraph (4) below) – per title
(i) where requested from a person's remote terminal and permitted in accordance with a notice given pursuant to rule 13 of the Land Registration (Open Register) Rules 1991 — £2
(ii) where requested by any other permitted means — £4

(4) Where permitted, inspection or office copy (or both) in relation to:

(a) a lease or mortgage referred to in the register, or a copy thereof; or
(b) any document not referred to in a register:

– per document — £8

(5) Application to the Registrar to ascertain the title number or numbers (if any) under which land is registered where the applicant seeks to inspect or to be supplied with an office copy of a register or part of a register or of a title plan and the applicant has not supplied a title number, or the title number supplied does not relate to any part of the land described by the applicant. — £4

PART III: Services – searches

Fee

(1) An official search with priority of the register or of a pending first registration application delivered to the Registrar by means of an applicant's remote terminal communicating with the Registrar's computer system where permitted in accordance with a notice given pursuant to r 14 of the Land Registration (Official Searches) Rules 1993 – per title — £2

FEES, DUTIES AND TAXES: 1 LAND REGISTRY FEES

(2)	An official search of the register by a mortgagee for the purpose of s 56(3) of the Family Law Act 1996 delivered to the Registrar by means of an applicant's remote terminal communicating with Registrar's computer system where permitted in accordance with a notice given pursuant to r 9 of the Land Registration (Matrimonial Home Rights) Rules 1997 – per title	£2
(3)	An official search of the register or of a pending first registration application other than as described in paragraphs (1) and (2) – per title	£4
(4)	A search of the register made by telephone	£4
(5)	The issue of an official certificate of inspection of the title plan	£4
(6)	Subject to art 10(4), an official search of the Index Map:	
	(a) where any part of the land to which the search relates is registered – per registered title in respect of which a result is given	£4
	(b) where no part of the land to which the search relates is registered – per application	£4
(7)	Official search of the index of proprietors' names – per name	£10

PART IV: Services – other information

		Fee
(1)	Application to be supplied with the name address of the registered proprietor of land identified by its postal address – per application	£4
(2)	The supply by the Registrar of a copy of an Index Map section – per copy	£40
(3)	The supply of information under section 129 of the Act – per registered title in respect of which information is supplied	£8
(4)	Application for day list information on any one occasion when a person gains access to the Registrar's computer system by means of that person's remote terminal pursuant to rule 4B of the Land Registration (Open Register) Rules 1991 – per title	£1

PART V: Services – miscellaneous

	Fee
To take an affidavit or declaration	£5
To take exhibits to an affidavit or declaration – per exhibit.	£2

THE CONVEYANCER'S FACTFINDER

FEES, DUTIES AND TAXES: 1 LAND REGISTRY FEES

1.4 Schedule 4 Exemptions

No fee shall be payable in respect of:

(1) making a land certificate or charge certificate correspond with the register;

(2) changing the name, address or description of a registered proprietor or other person referred to on the register, or changing the description of a property;

(3) giving effect on the register to a change of proprietor where the registered land or the registered charge, as the case may be, has become vested without further assurance (other than on the death or bankruptcy of a proprietor) in some person by the operation of any statute (other than the Act), statutory instrument or scheme taking effect under any statute or statutory instrument;

(4) registering the surrender of a registered lease (whether effected by deed or otherwise) where the surrender is consideration or part consideration for the grant of a new lease to the registered proprietor of substantially the same premises as were comprised in the surrendered lease and where a scale fee is paid for the registration of the new lease;

(5) registering a discharge of a registered charge;

(6) registering a notice or renewal of a caution or notice pursuant to the Family Law Act 1996;

(7) registering a withdrawal of a notice of deposit or intended deposit of a land certificate or charge certificate;

(8) entering on the register the death of a joint proprietor;

(9) registering a disposition to which s 145(2) of the Act (dispositions otherwise than for valuable consideration by personal representatives of a deceased proprietor registered as such) applies;

(10) registering a restriction which is obligatory under section 58(3) of the Act;

(11) cancelling the registration of a notice (other than a notice in respect of an unregistered lease or unregistered rentcharge), caution, inhibition, restriction or note;

(12) approving an estate layout plan or any draft document with or without a plan;

(13) issuing of a summons under the seal of the Land Registry;

(14) an order by the Registrar.

Stamp duty

2.1 Duty on the consideration for transfers or premises for lease from 28/03/2000

Consideration or premium	Rate of stamp duty
Up to £60,000: certified at £60,000	nil
£60,001 to £250,000: certified at £250,000	1%
£250,001 to £500,000: certified at £500,000	3%
Over £500,000	4%

Note 1: In calculating the consideration or premium, the amount is rounded up to a multiple of £5.

Note 2: A certificate of value for the appropriate amount must be included in the document to qualify for the lower rates of stamp duty.

Note 3: Where the consideration for a conveyance or transfer is not more than £150,000, check if the property is exempted from duty by the 'stamp duty exemption for disadvantaged areas', by telephoning the Inland Revenue helpline on 0845 603 0135 and giving the postcode of the property. See further **2.2** below.

2.2 Summary checklist – Disadvantaged areas stamp relief duty – Finance Act 2001, s 92
(issued by Inland Revenue – Stamp Taxes)

All instruments in respect of which relief is claimed must be formally adjudicated. To prevent delay in processing claims it will generally assist if all the following information is supplied at the time the instrument is presented for stamping:

- the document containing a certificate confirming it is within the provisions of s 92 of the Finance Act 2001;
- the full postcode of the property being transferred;
- the relevant PD form, if appropriate;
- a photocopy of the entire transfer document;
- a copy of the contract or sale agreement;
- the document containing a £250,000 certificate of title;
- if the document is a lease, a payment in respect of the rent element.

Provision of all the information above when the document is presented for stamping should enable claims to be processed without further correspondence.

If examination of the claim results in a decision that the relief under Finance Act 2002, s 92 is not due, and, as a consequence, payment of stamp duty is made after the proper time, a charge to interest may be incurred.

FEES, DUTIES AND TAXES: 2 STAMP DUTY

2.3 Duty on a lease at a rent only

Term of the lease	Rate of duty
Not more than 7 years:	
At a rent of £5,000 or less	nil
At a rent of more than £5,000	1%
More than 7 years but not more than 35 years	2%
More than 35 years but not more than 100 years	12%
Over 100 years	24%

Note 1: All amounts are rounded up to the next multiple of £5. (On leases where duty is payable on the rent and the premium the two amounts are added together before being rounded up.)

Note 2: Rent is 'the average annual rent'. It is calculated by aggregating the rent payable for each year of the term and dividing the total by the number of years of the term (including part years). If any part of the term has expired before the execution of the lease or agreement for the lease, that part should be omitted from the calculation.

2.4 The Stamp Duty (Exempt Instruments) Regulations 1987

(1) Certain documents dated ON OR AFTER 1 MAY 1987 will be exempt from stamp duty (subject to a certificate) and will no longer need to be seen in stamp offices, either for stamping or adjudication. Once certified, the documents can be sent straight to the Registrar or other person who may need to act upon them.

Instruments to which the Regulations apply

(2) The Regulations apply to conveyances or transfers of property of any description which fall within the exempt categories listed in the appendix. The conveyance or transfer is not excluded from the Regulations if it contains incidental matter that is not itself a transaction.

The certificate

(3) The certificate should be:

- included as part of the document or endorsed upon the document;
- firmly attached to the document (if prepared separately);
- signed by the transferor, grantor or solicitor on his or her behalf (an authorised agent of the transferor or grantor may also sign provided he or she is aware of the details on the certificate and states the capacity in which a certificate is given); and should include:
- the category into which the document falls; and
- a full description of the document where the certificate is on an attached sheet.

FEES, DUTIES AND TAXES: 2 STAMP DUTY

(4) A suggested form of words is

'I/WE HEREBY CERTIFY THAT THIS INSTRUMENT FALLS WITHIN CATEGORY .... IN THE SCHEDULE TO THE STAMP DUTY (EXEMPT INSTRUMENTS) REGULATIONS 1987'.

The exempt categories

A. The vesting of property subject to a trust in the trustees of the trust on the appointment of a new trustee, or in the continuing trustees on the retirement of a trustee.

B. The conveyance or transfer of property the subject of a specific devise or legacy to the beneficiary named in the will (or the nominee).

C. The conveyance or transfer of property which forms part of an intestate's estate to the person entitled on intestacy (or the nominee).

D. The appropriation of property within s 84(4) of the Finance Act 1985 (death: appropriation in satisfaction of a general legacy of money) or s 84(5) or (7) of that Act (death: appropriation in satisfaction or any interest of surviving spouse and in Scotland also of any interest of issue).

E. The conveyance or transfer of property which forms part of the residuary estate of a testator to a beneficiary (or the nominee) entitled solely by virtue of his or her entitlement under the will.

F. The conveyance or transfer of property out of a settlement in or towards satisfaction of a beneficiary's interest, not being an interest accrued for money or money's worth, being a conveyance or transfer constituting a distribution of property in accordance with the provisions of the settlement.

G. The conveyance or transfer of property on and in consideration only of marriage to a party to the marriage (or the nominee) or to trustees to be held on the terms of a settlement made in consideration only of the marriage.

H. The conveyance or transfer of property within s 83(1) of the Finance Act 1985 (for example, transfers in connection with divorce).

I. The conveyance or transfer by the liquidator of property which formed part of the assets of the company in liquidation to a shareholder of that company (or the nominee) in or towards satisfaction of the shareholder's rights on a winding up.

J. The grant in fee simple of an easement in or over the land for no consideration in money or money's worth.

K. The grant of a servitude for no consideration in money or money's worth.

L. The conveyance or transfer of property operating as a voluntary disposition *inter vivos* for no consideration in money or money's worth nor any consideration referred to in s 57 of the Stamp Act 1981 (conveyance in consideration of a debt).

M. The conveyance or transfer of property by an instrument within s 84(1) of the Finance Act 1985 (death: varying disposition).

THE CONVEYANCER'S FACTFINDER

Rates of tax and allowances 2002/03

3.1 Income tax

Rate of tax	Band of taxable income
Starting rate (10%)	£0 to £1,920
Basic rate (22%)	£1,921 to £29,900
Higher rate (40%)	over £29,900

3.2 Capital gains tax (CGT)

Annual exempt amount   £7,700

Husbands and wives are each entitled to their own £7,700 annual exempt amount.

For 2001/02, gains (after the deduction of allowable losses) below the starting rate limit will be taxed at 10%, gains between the starting rate and basic rate limits will be taxed at 20% and above the higher rate limit will be taxed at 40%.

3.3 Inheritance tax

Threshold   £250,000

No tax is payable if the total of all chargeable transfers is less than this threshold. Above this amount, tax is payable on the excess at a single rate of 40%.

Land charges fees and search fees

4.1 Land charges fees

The fees reproduced in this section are prescribed by the Land Charges Fees Rules 1990, SI 1990/327, which came into force on 2 April 1990.

Service	Amount of fee
Registration, renewal, rectification or cancellation of an entry in any register per name	£1
Certificate of cancellation per name	£1
Entry of priority notice per name	£1
Inspection of an entry in the register per entry	£1
Office copy of an entry in the register (including any plan) whether the application is made in writing or by telephone or teleprinter or fascimile transmission per copy	£1
Official search in the index (including issue of printed certificate of result):	written application per name £1 telephone application per name £2 facsimile transmission application per name £2
Official search in the index (including visual display of result of search and issue of printed certificate of such result)	per name £2

4.2 Local land charges search fees

The fees reproduced in this section are prescribed by the Local Land Charges (Amendment) Rules 1998, SI 1998/1190, which came into force on 1 June 1998.

Item	Fee
Registration of a charge in Part II of the register	£60
Filing a definitive certificate of the Lands Tribunal under rule 10(3)	£2.10
Filing a judgment, order or application for the variation or cancellation of an entry in Part II of the register	£6.30

FEES, DUTIES AND TAXES: 4 LAND CHARGES FEES AND SEARCH FEES

Inspection of documents filed under rule 10 in respect of each parcel of land	£2.10
Personal search	
(a) in the whole or in part of the register, and	£10
(b) in addition, in respect of each parcel of land above one, where under rule 11(3) the search extends to more than one parcel, subject to a maximum of £13	£1
Official search (including issue of official certificate of search):	
(a) in any one part of the register	£1.90
(b) in the whole of the register and	£5
(c) in addition, in respect of each parcel of land above one, where under rule 11(3) more than one parcel is included in the same requistion (whether the requisition is for a search in the whole or any part of the register), subject to a maximum of £13	£0.80
Office copy of any entry in the register (not including a copy or extract of any plan or document filed pursuant to these Rules)	£1.40
Office copy of any plan or other document filed pursuant to these Rules	Such reasonable fee as may be fixed by the registering authority according to the time and work involved.

4.3 Local authority search fees

Local authorities are empowered to make charges for answering enquiries about the exercise of their functions, where the enquiries are made in connection with land transactions. The amount of the charges is within the discretion of the local authority, but in determining the amount it must have regard to the costs of answering such enquiries.

See the Local Authorities (Charges for Land Searches) Regulations 1994, SI 1994/1885.

4.4 Commons search fees

The fees reproduced in this section are prescribed by the Commons Registration (General) (Amendment) Regulations 1989, SI 1989/2167.

Service	Fee
Official search and certificate	£6
Further fee in respect of each additional parcel of land included in the search	£0.50 (subject to a maximum of £10)

FEES, DUTIES AND TAXES: 4 LAND CHARGES FEES AND SEARCH FEES

Service	Fee
Certified copy of an entry or of an extract from any register map	Such reasonable fee as the registration authority may fix according to the time and labour involved

4.5 Coal mining report fees

The following fees came into force on 1 April 2001.

Type of enquiry	Total fee (including VAT at the standard rate)
Law Society Scheme Standard Search (Con29M enquiries 1 to 9 inclusive)	£15
Law Society Scheme Standard and Special Search (Con29M enquiries 1 to 12)	£23
Subsidence Damage Claim Search (Con29M enquiry 9 only)	£10
Non Scheme Standard Search Base Rate	£26
Expedited fee (payable in addition to total fee)	£59

REMINDERS: 5 STANDARD CONDITIONS OF SALE (THIRD EDITION)

To be printed under licence by the Law Society.

Standard Conditions of Sale (third edition)

5.1 **National Conditions of Sale 23rd edition, Law Society's Conditions of Sale 1995**

1 **General**

1.1 Definitions

    1.1.1 In these conditions:

    (a) 'accrued interest' means:

        (i) if money has been placed on deposit or in a building society share account, the interest actually earned

        (ii) otherwise, the interest which might reasonably have been earned by depositing the money at interest on seven days' notice of withdrawal with a clearing bank

        less, in either case, any proper charges for handling the money

    (b) 'agreement' means the contractual document which incorporates these conditions, with or without amendment

    (c) 'banker's draft' means a draft drawn by and on a clearing bank

    (d) 'clearing bank' means a bank which is a member of CHAPS Limited

    (e) 'completion date', unless defined in the agreement, has the meaning given in condition 6.1.1

    (f) 'contract' means the bargain between the seller and the buyer of which these conditions, with or without amendment, form part

    (g) 'contract rate', unless defined in the agreement, is the Law Society's interest rate from time to time in force

    (h) 'lease' includes sub-lease, tenancy and agreement for a lease or sub-lease

    (i) 'notice to complete' means a notice requiring completion of the contract in accordance with Condition 6

    (j) 'public requirement' means any notice, order or proposal given or made (whether before or after the date of the contract) by a body acting on statutory authority

    (k) 'requisition' includes objection

    (l) 'solicitor' includes barrister, duly certificated notary public, recognised licensed conveyancer and recognised body under sections 9 or 32 of the Administration of Justice Act 1985

REMINDERS: 5 STANDARD CONDITIONS OF SALE (THIRD EDITION)

    (m) 'transfer' includes conveyance and assignment

    (n) 'working day' means any day from Monday to Friday (inclusive) which is not Christmas Day, Good Friday or a statutory Bank Holiday.

1.1.2 When used in these conditions the terms 'absolute title' and 'office copies' have the special meaning given to them by the Land Registration Act 1925.

1.2 Joint parties

If there is more than one seller or more than one buyer, the obligations which they undertake can be enforced against them all jointly or against each individually.

1.3 Notices and documents

1.3.1 A notice required or authorised by the contract must be in writing.

1.3.2 Giving a notice or delivering a document to a party's solicitor has the same effect as giving or delivering it to that party.

1.3.3 Transmission by fax is a valid means of giving a notice or delivering a document where delivery of the original document is not essential.

1.3.4 Subject to conditions 1.3.5 to 1.3.7, a notice is given and a document delivered when it is received.

1.3.5 If a notice or document is received after 4.00pm on a working day, or on a day which is not a working day, it is to be treated as having been received on the next working day.

1.3.6 Unless the actual time of receipt is proved, a notice or document sent by the following means is to be treated as having been received before 4.00pm on the day shown below:

    (a) by first-class post: two working days after posting

    (b) by second-class post: three working days after posting

    (c) through a document exchange: on the first working day after the day on which it would normally be available for collection by the addressee.

1.3.7 Where a notice or document is sent through a document exchange, then for the purposes of condition 1.3.6 the actual time of receipt is:

    (a) the time when the addressee collects it from the document exchange or, if earlier

    (b) 8.00am on the first working day on which it is available for collection at that time.

1.4 VAT

1.4.1 An obligation to pay money includes an obligation to pay any value added tax chargeable in respect of that payment.

1.4.2 All sums made payable by the contract are exclusive of value added tax.

5 standard conditions of sale (third edition)

REMINDERS: 5 STANDARD CONDITIONS OF SALE (THIRD EDITION)

2 **Formation**

2.1 Date

2.1.1 If the parties intend to make a contract by exchanging duplicate copies by post or through a document exchange, the contract is made when the last copy is posted or deposited at the document exchange.

2.1.2 If the parties' solicitors agree to treat exchange as taking place before duplicate copies are actually exchanged, the contract is made as so agreed.

2.2 Deposit

2.2.1 The buyer is to pay or send a deposit of 10 per cent of the purchase price no later than the date of the contract. Except on a sale by auction, payment is to be made by banker's draft or by a cheque drawn on a solicitors' clearing bank account.

2.2.2 If before completion date the seller agrees to buy another property in England and Wales for his residence, he may use all or any part of the deposit as a deposit in that transaction to be held on terms to the same effect as this condition and condition 2.2.3.

2.2.3 Any deposit or part of a deposit not being used in accordance with condition 2.2.2 is to be held by the seller's solicitor as stakeholder on terms that on completion it is paid to the seller with accrued interest.

2.2.4 If a cheque tendered in payment of all or part of the deposit is dishonoured when first presented, the seller may, within seven working days of being notified that the cheque has been dishonoured, give notice to the buyer that the contract is discharged by the buyer's breach.

2.3 Auctions

2.3.1 On a sale by auction the following conditions apply to the property and, if it is sold in lots, to each lot.

2.3.2 The sale is subject to a reserve price.

2.3.3 The seller, or a person on his behalf, may bid up to the reserve price.

2.3.4 The auctioneer may refuse any bid.

2.3.5 If there is a dispute about a bid, the auctioneer may resolve the dispute or restart the auction at the last undisputed bid.

3 **Matters affecting the property**

3.1 Freedom from incumbrances

3.1.1 The seller is selling the property free from incumbrances, other than those mentioned in condition 3.1.2.

3.1.2 The incumbrances subject to which the property is sold are:

(a) those mentioned in the agreement

(b) those discoverable by inspection of the property before the contract

(c) those the seller does not and could not know about

(d) entries made before the date of the contract in any public register except those maintained by HM Land Registry or its Land Charges Department or by Companies House

(e) public requirements.

3.1.3 After the contract is made, the seller is to give the buyer written details without delay of any new public requirement and of anything in writing which he learns about concerning any incumbrances subject to which the property is sold.

3.1.4 The buyer is to bear the cost of complying with any outstanding public requirement and is to indemnify the seller against any liability resulting from a public requirement.

3.2 **Physical state**

3.2.1 The buyer accepts the property in the physical state it is in at the date of the contract unless the seller is building or converting it.

3.2.2 A leasehold property is sold subject to any subsisting breach of a condition or tenant's obligation relating to the physical state of the property which renders the lease liable to forfeiture.

3.2.3 A sublease is granted subject to any subsisting breach of a condition or tenant's obligation relating to the physical state of the property which renders the seller's own lease liable to forfeiture.

3.3 **Leases affecting the property**

3.3.1 The following provisions apply if the agreement states that any part of the property is sold subject to a lease.

3.3.2

(a) The seller having provided the buyer with full details of each lease or copies of the documents embodying the lease terms, the buyer is treated as entering into the contract knowing and fully accepting those terms

(b) The seller is to inform the buyer without delay if the lease ends or if the seller learns of any application by the tenant in connection with the lease; the seller is then to act as the buyer reasonably directs, and the buyer is to indemnify him against all consequent loss and expense

(c) The seller is not to agree to any proposal to change the lease terms without the consent of the buyer and is to inform the buyer without delay of any change which may be proposed or agreed

(d) The buyer is to indemnify the seller against all claims arising from the lease after actual completion; this includes claims which are unenforceable against a buyer for want of registration

(e) The seller takes no responsibility for what rent is lawfully recoverable, nor for whether or how any legislation affects the lease

(f) If the let land is not wholly within the property, the seller may apportion the rent.

3.4 Retained land

3.4.1 The following provisions apply where after the transfer the seller will be retaining land near the property.

3.4.2 The buyer will have no right of light or air over the retained land, but otherwise the seller and the buyer will each have the rights over the land of the other which they would have had if they were two separate buyers to whom the seller had made simultaneous transfers of the property and the retained land.

3.4.3 Either party may require that the transfer contain appropriate express terms.

4 Title and transfer

4.1 Timetable

4.1.1 The following are the steps for deducing and investigating the title to the property to be taken within the following time limits:

Step	Time limit
1. The seller is to send the buyer evidence of title in accordance with condition 4.2	Immediately after making the contract
2. The buyer may raise written requisitions	Six working days after either the date of the contract or the date of delivery of the seller's evidence of title on which the requisitions are raised whichever is the later
3. The seller is to reply in writing to any requisitions raised	Four working days after receiving the requisitions
4. The buyer may make written observations on the seller's replies	Three working days after receiving replies

The time limit on the buyer's right to raise requisitions applies even where the seller supplies incomplete evidence of his title, but the buyer may, within six working days from delivery of any further evidence, raise further requisitions resulting from that evidence. On the expiry of the relevant time limit the buyer loses his right to raise requisitions or make observations.

4.1.2 The parties are to take the following steps to prepare and agree the transfer of the property within the following time limits:

REMINDERS: 5 STANDARD CONDITIONS OF SALE (THIRD EDITION)

Step	Time limit
A. The buyer is to send the seller a draft transfer	At least twelve working days before completion date
B. The seller is to approve or revise that draft and either return it or retain it for use as the actual transfer	Four working days after delivery of the draft transfer
C. If the draft is returned the buyer is to send an engrossment to the seller	At least five working days before completion date

4.1.3 Periods of time under conditions 4.1.1 and 4.1.2 may run concurrently.

4.1.4 If the period between the date of the contract and completion date is less than 15 working days, the time limits in conditions 4.1.1 and 4.1.2 are to be reduced by the same proportion as that period bears to the period of 15 working days. Fractions of a working day are to be rounded down except that the time limit to perform any step is not to be less than one working day.

4.2 **Proof of title**

4.2.1 The evidence of registered title is office copies of the items required to be furnished by section 110(1) of the Land Registration Act 1925 and the copies, abstracts and evidence referred to in section 110(2).

4.2.2 The evidence of unregistered title is an abstract of the title, or an epitome of title with photocopies of the relevant documents.

4.2.3 Where the title to the property is unregistered, the seller is to produce to the buyer (without cost to the buyer):

(a) the original of every relevant document, or

(b) an abstract, epitome or copy with an original marking by a solicitor of examination either against the original or against an examined abstract or against an examined copy.

4.3 **Defining the property**

4.3.1 The seller need not:

(a) prove the exact boundaries of the property

(b) prove who owns fences, ditches, hedges or walls

(c) separately identify parts of the property with different titles further than he may be able to do from information in his possession.

4.3.2 The buyer may, if it is reasonable, require the seller to make or obtain, pay for and hand over a statutory declaration about facts relevant to the matters mentioned in condition 4.3.1. The form of the declaration is to be agreed by the buyer, who must not unreasonably withhold his agreement.

REMINDERS: 5 STANDARD CONDITIONS OF SALE (THIRD EDITION)

4.4 Rents and rent charges

The fact that a rent or rent charge, whether payable or receivable by the owner of the property, has been or will on completion be, informally apportioned is not to be regarded as a defect in title.

4.5 Transfer

4.5.1 The buyer does not prejudice his right to raise requisitions, or to require replies to any raised, by taking any steps in relation to the preparation or agreement of the transfer.

4.5.2 If the agreement makes no provision as to title guarantee, then subject to condition 4.5.3 the seller is to transfer the property with full title guarantee.

4.5.3 The transfer is to have effect as if the disposition is expressly made subject to all matters to which the property is sold subject under the terms of the contract.

4.5.4 If after completion the seller will remain bound by any obligation affecting the property, but the law does not imply any covenant by the buyer to indemnify the seller against liability for future breaches of it:

(a) the buyer is to covenant in the transfer to indemnify the seller against liability for any future breach of the obligation and to perform it from then on, and

(b) if required by the seller, the buyer is to execute and deliver to the seller on completion a duplicate transfer prepared by the buyer.

4.5.5 The seller is to arrange at his expense that, in relation to every document of title which the buyer does not receive on completion, the buyer is to have the benefit of:

(a) a written acknowledgement of his right to its production, and

(b) a written undertaking for its safe custody (except while it is held by a mortgagee or by someone in a fiduciary capacity).

5 Pending completion

5.1 Responsibility for property

5.1.1 The seller will transfer the property in the same physical state as it was at the date of the contract (except for fair wear and tear), which means that the seller retains the risk until completion.

5.1.2 If at any time before completion the physical state of the property makes it unusable for its purpose at the date of the contract:

(a) the buyer may rescind the contract

(b) the seller may rescind the contract where the property has become unusable for that purpose as a result of damage against which the seller could not reasonably have insured, or which it is not legally possible for the seller to make good.

5.1.3 The seller is under no obligation to the buyer to insure the property.

REMINDERS: 5 STANDARD CONDITIONS OF SALE (THIRD EDITION)

5.1.4 Section 47 of the Law of Property Act 1925 does not apply.

5.2 **Occupation by buyer**

5.2.1 If the buyer is not already lawfully in the property, and the seller agrees to let him into occupation, the buyer occupies on the following terms.

5.2.2 The buyer is a licensee and not a tenant. The terms of the licence are that the buyer:

(a) cannot transfer it

(b) may permit members of his household to occupy the property

(c) is to pay or indemnify the seller against all outgoings and other expenses in respect of the property

(d) is to pay the seller a fee calculated at the contract rate on the purchase price (less any deposit paid) for the period of the licence

(e) is entitled to any rents and profits from any part of the property which he does not occupy

(f) is to keep the property in as good a state of repair as it was in when he went into occupation (except for fair wear and tear) and is not to alter it

(g) is to insure the property in a sum which is not less than the purchase price against all risks in respect of which comparable premises are normally insured

(h) is to quit the property when the licence ends.

5.2.3 On the creation of the buyer's licence, condition 5.1 ceases to apply, which means that the buyer then assumes the risk until completion.

5.2.4 The buyer is not in occupation for the purposes of this condition if he merely exercises rights of access given solely to do work agreed by the seller.

5.2.5 The buyer's licence ends on the earliest of completion date, rescission of the contract or when five working days' notice given by one party to the other takes effect.

5.2.6 If the buyer is in occupation of the property after his licence has come to an end and the contract is subsequently completed he is to pay the seller compensation for his continued occupation calculated at the same rate as the fee mentioned in condition 5.2.2(d).

5.2.7 The buyer's right to raise requisitions is unaffected.

6 **Completion**

6.1 **Date**

6.1.1 Completion date is twenty working days after the date of the contract but time is not of the essence of the contract unless a notice to complete has been served.

6.1.2 If the money due on completion is received after 2.00pm, completion is to be treated, for the purposes only of conditions 6.3 and 7.3, as taking place on the next working day.

6.1.3 Condition 6.1.2 does not apply where the sale is with vacant possession of the property or any part and the seller has not vacated the property or that part by 2.00 pm on the date of actual completion.

6.2 Place

Completion is to take place in England and Wales, either at the seller's solicitor's office or at some other place which the seller reasonably specifies.

6.3 Apportionments

6.3.1 Income and outgoings of the property are to be apportioned between the parties so far as the change of ownership on completion will affect entitlement to receive or liability to pay them.

6.3.2 If the whole property is sold with vacant possession or the seller exercises his option in condition 7.3.4, apportionment is to be made with effect from the date of actual completion; otherwise, it is to be made from completion date.

6.3.3 In apportioning any sum, it is to be assumed that the seller owns the property until the end of the day from which apportionment is made and that the sum accrues from day to day at the rate at which it is payable on that day.

6.3.4 For the purpose of apportioning income and outgoings, it is to be assumed that they accrue at an equal daily rate throughout the year.

6.3.5 When a sum to be apportioned is not known or easily ascertainable at completion, a provisional apportionment is to be made according to the best estimate available. As soon as the amount is known, a final apportionment is to be made and notified to the other party. Any resulting balance is to be paid no more than ten working days later, and if not then paid the balance is to bear interest at the contract rate from then until payment.

6.3.6 Compensation payable under condition 5.2.6 is not to be apportioned.

6.4 Amount payable

The amount payable by the buyer on completion is the purchase price (less any deposit already paid to the seller or his agent) adjusted to take account of:

(a) apportionments made under condition 6.3

(b) any compensation to be paid or allowed under condition 7.3.

REMINDERS: 5 STANDARD CONDITIONS OF SALE (THIRD EDITION)

6.5 Title deeds

6.5.1 The seller is not to retain the documents of title after the buyer has tendered the amount payable under condition 6.4.

6.5.2 Condition 6.5.1 does not apply to any documents of title relating to land being retained by the seller after completion.

6.6 Rent receipts

The buyer is to assume that whoever gave any receipt for a payment of rent or service charge which the seller produces was the person or the agent of the person then entitled to that rent or service charge.

6.7 Means of payment

The buyer is to pay the money due on completion in one or more of the following ways:

(a) legal tender

(b) a banker's draft

(c) a direct credit to a bank account nominated by the seller's solicitor

(d) an unconditional release of a deposit held by a stakeholder.

6.8 Notice to complete

6.8.1 At any time on or after completion date, a party who is ready able and willing to complete may give the other a notice to complete.

6.8.2 A party is ready able and willing:

(a) if he could be, but for the default of the other party, and

(b) in the case of the seller, even though a mortgage remains secured on the property, if the amount to be paid on completion enables the property to be transferred freed of all mortgages (except those to which the sale is expressly subject).

6.8.3 The parties are to complete the contract within ten working days of giving a notice to complete, excluding the day on which the notice is given. For this purpose, time is of the essence of the contract.

6.8.4 On receipt of a notice to complete:

(a) if the buyer paid no deposit, he is forthwith to pay a deposit of 10 per cent

(b) if the buyer paid a deposit of less than 10 per cent, he is forthwith to pay a further deposit equal to the balance of that 10 per cent.

7 Remedies

7.1 Errors and omissions

7.1.1 If any plan or statement in the contract, or in the negotiations leading to it, is or was misleading or inaccurate due to an error or omission, the remedies available are as follows.

THE CONVEYANCER'S FACTFINDER 25

REMINDERS: 5 STANDARD CONDITIONS OF SALE (THIRD EDITION)

- 7.1.2 When there is a material difference between the description or value of the property as represented and as it is, the injured party is entitled to damages.
- 7.1.3 An error or omission only entitles the injured party to rescind the contract:
  - (a) where it results from fraud or recklessness, or
  - (b) where he would be obliged, to his prejudice, to transfer or accept property differing substantially (in quantity, quality or tenure) from what the error or omission had led him to expect.

7.2 Rescission

If either party rescinds the contract:

- (a) unless the rescission is a result of the buyer's breach of contract the deposit is to be repaid to the buyer with accrued interest
- (b) the buyer is to return any documents he received from the seller and is to cancel any registration of the contract.

7.3 Late completion

- 7.3.1 If there is default by either or both of the parties in performing their obligations under the contract and completion is delayed, the party whose total period of default is the greater is to pay compensation to the other party.
- 7.3.2 Compensation is calculated at the contract rate on the purchase price, or (where the buyer is the paying party) the purchase price less any deposit paid, for the period by which the paying party's default exceeds that of the receiving party, or, if shorter, the period between completion date and actual completion.
- 7.3.3 Any claim for loss resulting from delayed completion is to be reduced by any compensation paid under this contract.
- 7.3.4 Where the buyer holds the property as tenant of the seller and completion is delayed, the seller may give notice to the buyer, before the date of actual completion, that he intends to take the net income from the property until completion. If he does so, he cannot claim compensation under condition 7.3.1 as well.

7.4 After completion

Completion does not cancel liability to perform any outstanding obligation under this contract.

7.5 Buyer's failure to comply with notice to complete

- 7.5.1 If the buyer fails to complete in accordance with a notice to complete, the following terms apply.
- 7.5.2 The seller may rescind the contract, and if he does so:
  - (a) he may
    - (i) forfeit and keep any deposit and accrued interest

(ii) resell the property

(iii) claim damages

(b) the buyer is to return any documents he received from the seller and is to cancel any registration of the contract.

7.5.3 The seller retains his other rights and remedies.

7.6 Seller's failure to comply with notice to complete

7.6.1 If the seller fails to complete in accordance with a notice to complete, the following terms apply.

7.6.2 The buyer may rescind the contract, and if he does so:

(a) the deposit is to be repaid to the buyer with accrued interest

(b) the buyer is to return any documents he received from the seller and is, at the seller's expense, to cancel any registration of the contract.

7.6.3 The buyer retains his other rights and remedies.

8 Leasehold property

8.1 Existing leases

8.1.1 The following provisions apply to a sale of leasehold land.

8.1.2 The seller having provided the buyer with copies of the documents embodying the lease terms, the buyer is treated as entering into the contract knowing and fully accepting those terms.

8.1.3 The seller is to comply with any lease obligations requiring the tenant to insure the property.

8.2 New leases

8.2.1 The following provisions apply to a grant of a new lease.

8.2.2 The conditions apply so that:

'seller' means the proposed landlord

'buyer' means the proposed tenant

'purchase price' means the premium to be paid on the grant of a lease.

8.2.3 The lease is to be in the form of the draft attached to the agreement.

8.2.4 If the term of the new lease will exceed 21 years, the seller is to deduce a title which will enable the buyer to register the lease at HM Land Registry with an absolute title.

8.2.5 The buyer is not entitled to transfer the benefit of the contract.

8.2.6 The seller is to engross the lease and a counterpart of it and is to send the counterpart to the buyer at least five working days before completion date.

8.2.7 The buyer is to execute the counterpart and deliver it to the seller on completion.

REMINDERS: 5 STANDARD CONDITIONS OF SALE (THIRD EDITION)

8.3 Landlord's consent

8.3.1 The following provisions apply if a consent to assign or sub-let is required to complete the contract.

8.3.2

(a) The seller is to apply for the consent at his expense, and to use all reasonable efforts to obtain it

(b) The buyer is to provide all information and references reasonably required.

8.3.3 The buyer is not entitled to transfer the benefit of the contract.

8.3.4 Unless he is in breach of his obligation under condition 8.3.2, either party may rescind the contract by notice to the other party if three working days before completion date:

(a) the consent has not been given or

(b) the consent has been given subject to a condition to which the buyer reasonably objects.

In that case, neither party is to be treated as in breach of contract and condition 7.2 applies.

9 Chattels

9.1 The following provisions apply to any chattels which are to be sold.

9.2 Whether or not a separate price is to be paid for the chattels, the contract takes effect as a contract for sale of goods.

9.3 Ownership of the chattels passes to the buyer on actual completion.

CML Lenders' Handbook

6.1 The CML Lenders' Handbook for Solicitors and Licensed Conveyancers England and Wales (1999)

PART 1 - INSTRUCTIONS AND GUIDANCE

Those lenders who instruct using the CML Lenders' Handbook certify that these instructions have been prepared to comply with the requirements of Rule 6(3) of the Solicitors' Practice Rules 1990.

1. GENERAL

1.1 The CML Lenders' Handbook is issued by the Council of Mortgage Lenders. Your instructions from an individual lender will indicate if you are being instructed in accordance with the Lenders' Handbook. If you are, the general provisions in part 1 and any specific requirements in part 2 must be followed.

1.2 References to 'we' and 'our' means the lender from whom you receive instructions.

1.3 The Lenders' Handbook does not affect any responsibilities you have to us under the general law or any practice rule or guidance issued by your professional body from time to time.

1.4 The standard of care which we expect of you is that of a reasonably competent solicitor or licensed conveyancer acting on behalf of a mortgagee.

1.5 The limitations contained in rule 6(3)(c) and (e) of the Solicitors' Practice Rules 1990 apply to the instructions contained in the Lenders' Handbook and any separate instructions.

1.6 You must also comply with any separate instructions you receive for an individual loan.

1.7 If the borrower and the mortgagor are not one and the same person, all references to 'borrower' shall include the mortgagor.

1.8 References to 'borrower' (and, if applicable, 'guarantor' or, expressly or impliedly, the mortgagor) are to each borrower (and guarantor or mortgagor) named in the mortgage instructions/offer (if sent to the conveyancer). This applies to references in the Lenders' Handbook and in the certificate of title.

1.9 References to 'mortgage offer' include any loan agreement, offer of mortgage or any other similar document.

1.10 If you are instructed in connection with any additional loan (including a further advance) then you should treat references to 'mortgage' and 'mortgage offer' as applying to such 'additional loan' and 'additional loan offer' respectively.

REMINDERS: 6 CML LENDERS' HANDBOOK

1.11 In any transaction during the lifetime of the mortgage when we instruct you, you must use our current standard documents in all cases and must not amend them without our written consent. We will send you all the standard documents necessary to enable you to comply with our instructions, but please let us know if you need any other documents and we will send these to you. Check part 2 to see who you should contact. If you consider that any of the documentation is inappropriate to the particular facts of a transaction, you should write to us (see part 2) with full details and any suggested amendments.

1.12 In order to act on our behalf your firm must be a member of our conveyancing panel. You must also comply with any terms and conditions of your panel appointment.

1.13 If you or a member of your immediate family (that is to say, a spouse, co-habitee, parent, sibling, child, step-parent, step-child, grandparent, grandchild, parent-in-law, or child-in-law) is the borrower and you are a sole practitioner, you must not act for us.

1.14 Your firm or company must not act for us if the partner or fee earner dealing with the transaction or a member of his immediate family is the borrower, unless we say your firm may act (see part 2) and a separate fee earner of no less standing or a partner within the firm acts for us.

1.15 If there is any conflict of interest, you must not act for us and must return our instructions.

1.16 Nothing in these instructions lessens your duties to the borrower.

2. COMMUNICATIONS

2.1 All communications between you and us should be in writing quoting the mortgage account or roll number, the surname and initials of the borrower and the property address. You should keep copies of all written communication on your file as evidence of notification and authorisation. If you use PC fax or e-mail, you should keep a paper copy.

2.2 If you require deeds or information from us in respect of a borrower or a property then you must first of all have the borrower's authority for such a request. If there is more than one borrower, you must have the authority of all the borrowers.

2.3 If you need to report a matter to us, you must do so as soon as you become aware of it so as to avoid any delay. If you do not believe that a matter is adequately provided for in the Handbook, you should identify the relevant Handbook provision and the extent to which the issue is not covered by it. You should provide a concise summary of the legal risks and your recommendation on how we should protect our interest. After reporting a matter you should not complete the mortgage until you have received our further written instructions. We recommend that you report such matters before exchange of contracts because we may have to withdraw or change the mortgage offer.

REMINDERS: 6 CML LENDERS' HANDBOOK

3. **SAFEGUARDS**

3.1 You must follow the guidance in the Law Society's Green Card (mortgage fraud) and Pink Card (undertakings) and, to the extent that they apply, comply with the Money Laundering Regulations 1993 (see the Law Society's Blue Card). Licensed conveyancers must follow any guidance issued by the Council for Licensed Conveyancers.

3.2 If you are not familiar with the seller's solicitors or licensed conveyancers, you must verify that they appear in a legal directory or they are currently on record with the Law Society or Council for Licensed Conveyancers as practising at the address shown on their note paper.

3.3 Unless you personally know the signatory of a document, you must ask the signatory to provide evidence of identity, which you must carefully check. You should check the signatory's identity against one of the documents from list A or two of the documents in list B:

List A

- a valid full passport; or
- a valid H M Forces identity card with the signatory's photograph; or
- a valid UK Photo-card driving licence; or
- any other document listed in the additional list A in part 2.

List B

- a cheque guarantee card, credit card (bearing the Mastercard or Visa logo) American Express or Diners Club card, debit or multi-function card (bearing the Switch or Delta logo) issued in the United Kingdom with an original account statement less than three months old; or
- a firearm and shot gun certificate; or
- a receipted utility bill less than three months old; or
- a council tax bill less than three months old; or
- a council rent book showing the rent paid for the last three months; or
- a mortgage statement from another lender for the mortgage accounting year just ended; or
- any other document listed in the additional list B in part 2.

You should check that any document you use to verify a signatory's identity appears to be authentic and current, signed in the relevant place. You should take a copy of it and keep the copy on your file. You should also check that the signatory's signature on any document being used to verify identity matches the signatory's signature on the document we require the signatory to sign and that the address shown on any document used to verify identity is that of the signatory

3.4 All your duties to us under the Lenders' Handbook in relation to identifying signatories of documents will be satisfied by you complying with paragraphs 3.1, 3.2 and 3.3.

REMINDERS: CML LENDERS' HANDBOOK

4 VALUATION OF THE PROPERTY

4.1 Valuation

4.1.1 Check part 2 to see whether we send you a copy of the valuation report or if you must get it from the borrower. If you are sent, or are required to obtain, a copy of the valuation report:

4.1.1.1 you must take reasonable steps to verify that there are no discrepancies between the description of the property as valued and the title and other documents which a reasonably competent conveyancer should obtain, and, if there are, you must tell us immediately; and

4.1.1.2 you should take reasonable steps to verify that the assumptions stated by the valuer about the title (for example, its tenure, easements, boundaries and restrictions on its use) in the valuation are correct. If they are not, please let us know as soon as possible (see part 2) as it will be necessary for us to check with the valuer whether the valuation needs to be revised. We are not expecting you to assume the role of valuer.

We are simply trying to ensure that the valuer has valued the property based on correct information.

4.1.2 We recommend that you should advise the borrower that there may be defects in the property which are not revealed by the inspection carried out by our valuer and there may be omissions or inaccuracies in the report which do not matter to us but which would matter to the borrower. We recommend that, if we send a copy of a valuation report that we have obtained, you should also advise the borrower that the borrower should not rely on the report in deciding whether to proceed with the purchase and that he obtains his own more detailed report on the condition and value of the property, based on a fuller inspection, to enable him to decide whether the property is suitable for his purposes.

4.2 Re-inspection

Where the mortgage offer states that a final inspection is needed, you must ask for the final inspection at least 10 working days before the advance is required. Failure to do so may cause delay in the issue of the advance. Your certificate of title must be sent to us in the usual way (see part 2).

5. TITLE

5.1 Surrounding Circumstances

5.1.1 Please report to us (see part 2) if the owner or registered proprietor has been registered for less than six months or the person selling to the borrower is not the owner or registered proprietor unless the seller is:

5.1.1.1 a personal representative of the registered proprietor; or

5.1.1.2 an institutional mortgagee exercising its power of sale; or

REMINDERS: 6 CML LENDERS' HANDBOOK

5.1.1.3 a receiver, trustee-in-bankruptcy or liquidator; or

5.1.1.4 developer or builder selling a property acquired under a part-exchange scheme.

5.1.2 If any matter comes to the attention of the fee earner dealing with the transaction which you should reasonably expect us to consider important in deciding whether or not to lend to the borrower (such as whether the borrower has given misleading information to us or the information which you might reasonably expect to have been given to us is no longer true) and you are unable to disclose that information to us because of a conflict of interest, you must cease to act for us and return our instructions stating that you consider a conflict of interest has arisen.

5.2 Searches and Reports

5.2.1 In carrying out your investigation, you must make all usual and necessary searches and enquiries. We must be named as the applicant in the Land Registry search.

5.2.2 In addition, you must carry out any other searches which may be appropriate to the particular property, taking into account its locality and other features (see also paragraph 5.2.5).

5.2.3 All searches except where there is a priority period must not be more than six months old at completion.

5.2.4 You must make a mining search (such as a coal, tin, china clay or brine search) where it is reasonable to believe that the property could be affected by underground workings. The search must not be more than six months old at completion. In the case of a coal mining search, if the results of the search from the Coal Authority are such that the property is not affected by any of the matters mentioned in the report then we do not need to be notified of its contents. Subject to that, you should advise us if any entries are revealed in the same way as you would advise the borrower. You should not simply send us a copy of the mining search.

5.2.5 You must advise us of any contaminated land entries revealed in the local authority search. Check part 2 to see if we want to receive environmental or contaminated land reports (as opposed to contaminated land entries revealed in the local authority search). If we do not, you do not need to make these enquiries on our behalf.

5.2.6 For local authority searches under pararagraph 5.2.1, check part 2 to see if we accept:

5.2.6.1 personal searches; or

5.2.6.2 searches carried out by private search organisations; or

5.2.6.3 search insurance.

5.2.7 If we do accept personal searches, searches carried out by private search organisations or search insurance, you must ensure:

REMINDERS: 6 CML LENDERS' HANDBOOK

5.2.7.1 a suitably qualified search agent carries out the personal search and has indemnity insurance that adequately protects us; or

5.2.7.2 the private search organisation's indemnity insurance adequately protects us; or

5.2.7.3 the search insurance policy adequately protects us.

You must be satisfied that you will be able to certify that the title is good and marketable.

5.3 **Planning and Building Regulations**

5.3.1 You must by making appropriate searches and enquiries take all reasonable steps (including any further enquiries to clarify any issues which may arise) to ensure:

5.3.1.1 the property has the benefit of any necessary planning consents; and

5.3.1.2 there is no evidence of any breach of the conditions of that or any other consent or certificate affecting the property; and

5.3.1.3 that no matter is revealed which would preclude the property from being used as a residential property or that the property may be the subject of enforcement action.

5.3.2 If there is such evidence and the seller (or the borrower in the case of a remortgage) is not providing a sufficient undertaking to satisfy those outstanding conditions by completion, then this must be reported to us (see part 2). Check part 2 to see if copies of planning permissions, building regulations and other consents or certificates should be sent to us.

5.3.3 If the property will be subject to any enforceable restrictions, for example under an agreement (such as an agreement under section 106 of the Town and Country Planning Act 1990) or in a planning permission, which, at the time of completion, might reasonably be expected materially to affect its value or its future marketability, you should report this to us (see part 2).

5.4 **Good and Marketable Title**

5.4.1 The title to the property must be good and marketable free of any restrictions, covenants, easements, charges or encumbrances which, at the time of completion, might reasonably be expected to materially adversely affect the value of the property or its future marketability (but excluding any matters covered by indemnity insurance) and which may be accepted by us for mortgage purposes. Our requirements in respect of indemnity insurance are set out in paragraph 9. You must also take reasonable steps to ensure that, on completion, the property will be vested in the borrower.

5.4.2 Good leasehold title will be acceptable if:

REMINDERS: 6 CML LENDERS' HANDBOOK

5.4.2.1 a marked abstract of the freehold and any intermediate leasehold title for the statutory period of 15 years before the grant of the lease is provided; or

5.4.2.2 you are prepared to certify that the title is good and marketable when sending your certificate of title (because, for example, the landlord's title is generally accepted in the district where the property is situated); or

5.4.2.3 you arrange indemnity insurance. Our requirements in respect of indemnity insurance are set out in paragraph 9.

5.4.3 A title based on adverse possession or possessory title will be acceptable if:

5.4.3.1 there is satisfactory evidence by statutory declaration of adverse possession for a period of at least 12 years. In the case of lost title deeds, the statutory declaration must explain the loss satisfactorily;

5.4.3.2 we will also require indemnity insurance where there are buildings on the part in question or where the land is essential for access or services;

5.4.3.3 we may not need indemnity insurance in cases where such title affects land on which no buildings are erected or which is not essential for access or services. In such cases, you must send a plan of the whole of the land to be mortgaged to us identifying the area of land having possessory title. We will refer the matter to our valuer so that an assessment can be made of the proposed security. We will then notify you of any additional requirements or if a revised mortgage offer is to be made.

5.5 **Flying Freeholds, Freehold Flats and other Freehold Arrangements**

5.5.1 If any part of the property comprises or is affected by a flying freehold or the property is a freehold flat, check part 2 to see if we will accept it as security.

5.5.2 If we are prepared to accept a title falling within 5.5.1:

5.5.2.1 (unless we tell you not to in part 2) you must report to us that the property is a freehold flat or flying freehold; and

5.5.2.2 the property must have all necessary rights of support, protection, and entry for repair as well as a scheme of enforceable covenants that are also such that subsequent buyers are required to enter into covenants in identical form; and

5.5.2.3 you must be able to certify that the title is good and marketable; and

5.5.2.4 in the case of flying freeholds, you must send us a plan of the property clearly showing the part affected by the flying freehold.

If our requirements in 5.5.2.2 are not satisfied, indemnity must be in place at completion (see paragraph 9).

REMINDERS: 6 CML LENDERS' HANDBOOK

Other freehold arrangements

5.5.3 Unless we indicate to the contrary (see part 2), we have no objection to a security which comprises a building converted into not more than four flats where the borrower occupies one of those flats and the borrower or another flat owner also owns the freehold of the building and the other flats are subject to long leases.

    5.5.3.1 If the borrower occupying one of the flats also owns the freehold, we will require our security to be:

        5.5.3.1.1 the freehold of the whole building subject to the long leases of the other flats; and

        5.5.3.1.2 any leasehold interest the borrower will have in the flat the borrower is to occupy.

    5.5.3.2 If another flat owner owns the freehold of the building, the borrower must have a leasehold interest in the flat the borrower is to occupy and our security must be the borrower's leasehold interest in such flat.

    5.5.3.3 The leases of all the flats should contain appropriate covenants by the tenant of each flat to contribute towards the repair, maintenance and insurance of the building. The leases should also grant and reserve all necessary rights and easements. They should not contain any unduly onerous obligations on the landlord.

5.5.4 Where the security will comprise:

    5.5.4.1 one of a block of not more than four leasehold flats and the borrower will also own the freehold jointly with one or more of the other flat owners in the building; or

    5.5.4.2 one of two leasehold flats in a building where the borrower also owns the freehold reversion of the other flat and the other leaseholder owns the freehold reversion in the borrower's flat; check part 2 to see if we will accept it as security and if so, what our requirements will be.

5.6 Restrictions on Use and Occupation

You must check whether there are any material restrictions on the occupation of the property as a private residence or as specified by us (for example, because of the occupier's employment, age or income), or any material restrictions on its use. If there are any restrictions, you must report details to us (see part 2). In some cases, we may accept a restriction, particularly if this relates to sheltered housing or to first time buyers.

5.7 Restrictive Covenants

5.7.1 You must enquire whether the property has been built, altered or is currently used in breach of a restrictive covenant. We rely on you to check that the covenant is not enforceable. If you are unable to provide an unqualified certificate of title as a result of the risk of enforceability you must ensure

REMINDERS: 6 CML LENDERS' HANDBOOK

(subject to paragraph 5.7.2) that indemnity insurance is in place at completion of our mortgage (see paragraph 9).

5.7.2 We will not insist on indemnity insurance:

5.7.2.1 if you are satisfied that there is no risk to our security; and

5.7.2.2 the breach has continued for more than 20 years; and

5.7.2.3 there is nothing to suggest that any action is being taken or is threatened in respect of the breach.

5.8 First Legal Charge

On completion, we require a fully enforceable first charge by way of legal mortgage over the property executed by all owners of the legal estate. All existing charges must be redeemed on or before completion, unless we agree that an existing charge may be postponed to rank after our mortgage. Our standard deed or form of postponement must be used.

5.9 Other Loans

You must ask the borrower how the balance of the purchase price is being provided. If you become aware that the borrower is not providing the balance of the purchase price from his own funds and/or is proposing to give a second charge over the property, you must report this to us if the borrower agrees (see part 2), failing which you must return our instructions and explain that you are unable to continue to act for us as there is a conflict of interest.

5.10 Leasehold Property

5.10.1 Our requirements on the unexpired term of a lease offered as security are set out in part 2.

5.10.2 There must be no provision for forfeiture on the insolvency of the tenant or any superior tenant.

5.10.3 The only situations where we will accept a restriction on the mortgage or assignment (whether by a tenant or a mortgagee) of the lease is where the person whose consent needs to be obtained cannot unreasonably withhold giving consent. The necessary consent for the particular transaction must be obtained before completion. If the lease requires consent to an assignment or mortgage to be obtained, you must obtain these on or before completion (this is particularly important if the lease is a shared ownership lease). You must not complete without them.

5.10.4 You must take reasonable steps to check that:

5.10.4.1 there are satisfactory legal rights, particularly for access, services, support, shelter and protection; and

5.10.4.2 there are also adequate covenants and arrangements in respect of the following matters, buildings insurance, maintenance and repair of the structure, foundations, main walls, roof, common parts, common services and grounds (the 'common services').

5.10.5 You should ensure that responsibility for the insurance, maintenance and repair of the common services is that of:

5.10.5.1 the landlord; or

5.10.5.2 one or more of the tenants in the building of which the property forms part; or

5.10.5.3 the management company - see paragraph 5.11.

5.10.6 Where the responsibility for the insurance, maintenance and repair of the common services is that of one or more of the tenants;

5.10.6.1 the lease must contain adequate provisions for the enforcement of these obligations by the landlord or management company at the request of the tenant.

5.10.6.2 In the absence of a provision in the lease that all leases of other flats in the block are in, or will be granted in, substantially similar form, you should take reasonable steps to check that the leases of the other flats are in similar form. If you are unable to do so, you should effect indemnity insurance (see paragraph 9). This is not essential if the landlord is responsible for the maintenance and repair of the main structure.

5.10.6.3 We do not require enforceability covenants mutual or otherwise for other tenant covenants.

5.10.7 We have no objection to a lease which contains provision for a periodic increase of the ground rent provided that the amount of the increased ground rent is fixed or can be readily established and is reasonable. If you consider any increase in the ground rent may materially affect the value of the property, you must report this to us (see part 2).

5.10.8 You should enquire whether the landlord or managing agent foresees any significant increase in the level of the service charge in the reasonably foreseeable future and, if there is, you must report to us (see part 2).

5.10.9 If the terms of the lease are unsatisfactory, you must obtain a suitable deed of variation to remedy the defect. We may accept indemnity insurance (see paragraph 9). See part 2 for our requirements.

5.10.10 You must obtain on completion a clear receipt or other appropriate written confirmation for the last payment of ground rent and service charge from the landlord or managing agents on behalf of the landlord. Check part 2 to see if it must be sent to us after completion. If confirmation of payment from the landlord cannot be obtained, we are prepared to proceed provided that you are satisfied that the absence of the landlord is common practice in the district where the property is situated, the seller confirms there are no breaches of the terms of the lease, you are satisfied that our security will not be prejudiced by the absence of such a receipt and you provide us with a clear certificate of title.

REMINDERS: 6 CML LENDERS' HANDBOOK

5.10.11 Notice of the mortgage must be served on the landlord and any management company immediately following completion, whether or not the lease requires it. If you cannot obtain receipt of the notice then, as a last resort, suitable evidence of the service of the notice on the landlord should be provided. Check part 2 to see if a receipted copy of the notice or evidence of service must be sent to us after completion.

5.10.12 We will accept leases which require the property to be sold on the open market if re-building or reinstatement is frustrated provided the insurance proceeds and the proceeds of sale are shared between the landlord and tenant in proportion to their respective interests.

5.10.13 You must report to us (see part 2) if it becomes apparent that the landlord is either absent or insolvent. If we are to lend, we may require indemnity insurance (see paragraph 9). See part 2 for our requirements.

5.10.14 If the leasehold title is registered but the lease has been lost, we are prepared to proceed provided you have checked an M Land Registry produced copy of the registered lease. Whilst this will not be an office copy of the lease you may accept it as sufficient evidence of the lease and its terms when approving the title for mortgage purposes provided it is, on its face, a complete copy.

5.11 Management Company

5.11.1 In paragraph 5.11 the meanings shall apply:

- 'management company' means the company formed to carry out the maintenance and repair of the common parts;
- 'common parts' means the structure, main walls, roof, foundations, services grounds and any other common areas serving the building or estate of which the property forms part.

If a management company is required to maintain or repair the common parts, the management company should have a legal right to enter the property; if the management company's right to so enter does not arise from a leasehold interest, then the tenants of the building should also be the members of the management company.

If this is not the case, there should be a covenant by the landlord to carry out the obligations of the management company should it fail to do so.

5.11.1.1 For leases granted before 1 September 2000:

If the lease does not satisfy the requirements of paragraph 5.11.1 but: you are nevertheless satisfied that the existing arrangements affecting the management company and the maintenance and repair of the common parts are sufficient to ensure the adequate maintenance and repair of the common parts; and you are able to provide a clear certificate of title, then we will rely on your professional judgement.

5.11.2 You should make a company search and verify that the company is in existence and registered at Companies House. You should also obtain the management company's last three years' published accounts (or the accounts from inception if the company has only been formed in the past three years). Any apparent problems with the company should be reported to us (see part 2). If the borrower is required to be a shareholder in the management company, check part 2 to see if you must arrange for the share certificate, a blank stock transfer form executed by the borrower and a copy of the memorandum and articles of association to be sent to us after completion (unless we tell you not to). If the management company is limited by guarantee, the borrower (or at least one of them if two or more) must become a member on or before completion.

5.12 Insolvency Considerations

5.12.1 You must obtain a clear bankruptcy search against each borrower (and each mortgagor or guarantor, if any) providing us with protection at the date of completion of the mortgage. You must fully investigate any entries revealed by your bankruptcy search against the borrower (or mortgagor or guarantor) to ensure that they do not relate to them.

5.12.2 Where an entry is revealed against the name of the borrower (or the mortgagor or guarantor):

5.12.2.1 you must certify that the entry does not relate to the borrower (or the mortgagor or guarantor) if you are able to do so from your own knowledge or enquiries; or

5.12.2.2 if, after obtaining office copy entries or making other enquiries of the Official Receiver, you are unable to certify that the entry does not relate to the borrower (or the mortgagor or guarantor) you must report this to us (see part 2). We may as a consequence need to withdraw our mortgage offer.

5.12.3 If you are aware that the title to the property is subject to a deed of gift or a transaction at an apparent undervalue completed within five years of the proposed mortgage then you must be satisfied that we will acquire our interest in good faith and will be protected under the provisions of the Insolvency (No 2) Act 1994 against our security being set aside. If you are unable to give an unqualified certificate of title, you must arrange indemnity insurance (see paragraph 9).

5.12.4 You must also obtain clear bankruptcy searches against all parties to any deed of gift or transaction at an apparent undervalue.

5.13 Powers of Attorney

5.13.1 If any document is being executed under power of attorney, you must ensure that the power of attorney is, on its face, properly drawn up, that it appears to be properly executed by the donor and that the attorney knows of no reason why such power of attorney will not be subsisting at completion. Where there are joint borrowers the power should comply with section 25 of the Trustee Act 1925, as amended by section 7 of the Trustee Delegation Act 1999, or with section 1 of the Trustee Delegation Act 1999 with the attorney making an appropriate statement under section 2 of the 1999 Act. In the case of joint borrowers, neither borrower may appoint the other as attorney.

5.13.2 A power of attorney must not be used in connection with a regulated loan under the Consumer Credit Act 1974.

5.13.3 Check part 2 to see if:

5.13.3.1 the original or a certified copy of the power of attorney must be sent to us after completion;

5.13.3.2 where the power of attorney is a general power of attorney and was completed more than 12 months before the completion of our mortgage, you must send us a statutory declaration confirming that it has not been revoked.

5.14 Title Guarantee

Whilst we recommend that a borrower should try to obtain a full title guarantee from the seller, we do not insist on this. We, however, require the borrower to give us a full title guarantee in the mortgage deed. The mortgage deed must not be amended.

6. THE PROPERTY

6.1 Mortgage Offer and Title Documents

6.1.1 The loan to the borrower will not be made until all relevant conditions of the mortgage offer which need to be satisfied before completion have been complied with and we have received your certificate of title.

6.1.2 You must check your instructions and ensure that there are no discrepancies between them and the title documents and other matters revealed by your investigations.

6.1.3 You should tell us (see part 2) as soon as possible if you have been told that the borrower has decided not to take up the mortgage offer.

6.2 Boundaries

These must be clearly defined by reference to a suitable plan or description. They must also accord with the information given in the valuation report, if this is provided to you. You should check with the borrower that the plan or the description accords with the borrower's understanding of the extent of the property to be mortgaged to us. You must report to us (see part 2), if there are any discrepancies.

REMINDERS: 6 CML LENDERS' HANDBOOK

6.3 Purchase Price

6.3.1 The purchase price for the property must be the same as set out in our instructions. If it is not, you must tell us (unless we say differently in part 2). You must tell us (unless we say differently in part 2) if the contract provides for:

6.3.1.1 a cashback to the buyer; or

6.3.1.2 part of the price is being satisfied by a non-cash incentive to the buyer. This may lead to the mortgage offer being withdrawn or amended.

6.3.2 You must report to us (see part 2) if you will not have control over the payment of all of the purchase money (for example, if it is proposed that the borrower pays money to the seller direct) other than a deposit held by an estate agent or a reservation fee of not more than £500 paid to a builder or developer.

6.4 Vacant Possession

Unless otherwise stated in your instructions, it is a term of the loan that vacant possession is obtained. The contract must provide for this. If you doubt that vacant possession will be given, you must not part with the advance and should report the position to us (see part 2).

6.5 Properties Let At Completion

6.5.1 Where the property, or part of it, is already let, or is to be let at completion, then the letting must comply with the details set out in the mortgage offer or any consent to let we issue. If no such details are mentioned, you must report the position to us (see part 2).

6.5.2 Check part 2 for whether counterparts or certified copies of all tenancy agreements and leases in respect of existing tenancies must be sent to us after completion.

6.6 New Properties - Building Standards Indemnity Schemes

6.6.1 If the property is newly built, or newly converted, or to be occupied for the first time, you must ensure that it was built or converted under whichever of the following is acceptable to us (see part 2):

6.6.1.1 the National House-Building Council (NHBC) Buildmark scheme; or

6.6.1.2 the Zurich Municipal Newbuild scheme; or

6.6.1.3 Zurich Municipal Rebuild scheme; or

6.6.1.4 the Housing Association Property Mutual (HAPM) scheme; or

6.6.1.5 the Premier Guarantee for Private Housing and Completed Housing; or

6.6.1.6 any other new home warranty schemes.

REMINDERS: 6 CML LENDERS' HANDBOOK

6.6.2   Check part 2 to see what new home warranty documentation should be sent to us after completion.

6.6.3   We do not insist that notice of assignment of the benefit of the new home warranty agreement be given to the builder in the case of a second and subsequent purchase(s) during the period of the insurance cover. Check part 2 to see if any assignments of building standards indemnity schemes which are available should be sent to us after completion.

6.6.4   Check part 2 to see if we will accept the monitoring of a newly built or newly converted property to be occupied for the first time by a professional consultant. You should ensure that the professional consultant properly completes the lender's Professional Consultant's Certificate which forms an appendix to this Handbook or such other form as the instructing lender may provide. The professional consultant should also confirm to you that he has appropriate experience in the design or monitoring of the construction or conversion of residential buildings and has one or more of the following qualifications:

6.6.4.1   fellow or member of the Royal Institution of Chartered Surveyors (FRICS or MRICS); or

6.6.4.2   fellow or member of the Institution of Structural Engineers (F.I.Struct.E or M.I.Struct.E); or

6.6.4.3   fellow or member of the Chartered Institute of Building (FCIOB or MCIOB); or

6.6.4.4   fellow or member of the Architecture and Surveying Institute (FASI or MASI); or

6.6.4.5   fellow or member of the Association of Building Engineers (FB.Eng or MB.Eng); or

6.6.4.6   member of the British Institute of Architectural Technologists (MBIAT); or

6.6.4.7   architect registered with the Architects Registration Board (ARB). An architect must be registered with the Architects Registration Board, even if also a member of another institution, for example the Royal Institute of British Architects (RIBA); or

6.6.4.8   fellow or member of the Institution of Civil Engineers (FICE or MICE).

6.6.5   At the time he issues his certificate of practical completion, the consultant must have professional indemnity insurance in force for each claim for the greater of either:

6.6.5.1   the value of the property once completed; or

6.6.5.2   £250,000 if employed directly by the borrower or, in any other case, £500,000.

If we require a collateral warranty from any professional adviser, this will be stated specifically in the mortgage instructions.

6.6.6 Check part 2 to see if the consultant's certificate must be sent to us after completion.

6.7 Roads and Sewers

6.7.1 If the roads or sewers immediately serving the property are not adopted or maintained at public expense, there must be a suitable agreement and bond in existence or you must report to us (see part 2 for who you should report to).

6.7.2 If there is any such agreement, it should be secured by bond or deposit as required by the appropriate authority to cover the cost of making up the roads and sewers to adoptable standards, maintaining them thereafter and procuring adoption.

6.7.3 If there is an arrangement between the developer and the lender whereby the lender will not require a retention, you must obtain confirmation from the developer that the arrangement is still in force.

6.8 Easements

6.8.1 You must take all reasonable steps to check that the property has the benefit of all easements necessary for its full use and enjoyment. This would include, for example, rights of way (both vehicular and pedestrian), the use of services and any necessary rights of entry for repair. All such rights must be enforceable by the borrower and the borrower's successors in title. If they are not, you must report to us (see part 2).

6.8.2 If the borrower owns adjoining land over which the borrower requires access to the property or in respect of which services are provided to the property, this land must also be mortgaged to us.

6.9 Release of Retentions

6.9.1 If we make a retention from an advance (for example, for repairs, improvements or road works) we are not obliged to release that retention, or any part of it, if the borrower is in breach of any of his obligations under the mortgage, or if a condition attached to the retention has not been met or if the loan has been repaid in full. You should, therefore not give an unqualified undertaking to pay the retention to a third party.

6.9.2 Check part 2 to see who we will release the retention to.

6.10 Neighbourhood Changes

The local search or the enquiries of the seller or the seller's conveyancer should not reveal that the property is in an area scheduled for redevelopment or in any way affected by road proposals. If it is, please report this to us (see part 2).

REMINDERS: 6 CML LENDERS' HANDBOOK

6.11 Rights of Pre-emption and Restrictions on Resale

You must ensure that there are no rights of pre-emption, restrictions on resale, options or similar arrangements in existence at completion which will affect our security. If there are, please report this to us (see part 2).

6.12 Improvement and Repair Grants

Where the property is subject to an improvement or repair grant which will not be discharged or waived on completion, check part 2 to see whether you must report the matter to us.

6.13 Insurance

Where we do not arrange the insurance, you must:

6.13.1 report to us (see part 2) if the property is not insured in accordance with our requirements (one of our requirements, see part 2, will relate to whether the property is insured in the joint names of us and the borrower or whether our interest may be noted);

6.13.2 arrange that the insurance cover starts from no later than completion;

6.13.3 check that the amount of buildings insurance cover is at least the amount referred to in the mortgage offer (if the property is part of a larger building and there is a common insurance policy, the total sum insured for the building must be not less than the total number of flats multiplied by the amount set out in the mortgage offer for the property);

6.13.4 ensure that the buildings insurance cover is index linked;

6.13.5 ensure that the excess does not exceed the amount set out in part 2;

6.13.6 Check part 2 to see if we require you to confirm that all the following risks are covered in the insurance policy:

    6.13.6.1 fire;

    6.13.6.2 lightning;

    6.13.6.3 aircraft;

    6.13.6.4 explosion;

    6.13.6.5 earthquake;

    6.13.6.6 storm;

    6.13.6.7 flood;

    6.13.6.8 escape of water or oil;

    6.13.6.9 riot;

    6.13.6.10 malicious damage;

    6.13.6.11 theft or attempted theft;

REMINDERS: 6 CML LENDERS' HANDBOOK

    6.13.6.12 falling trees and branches and aerials;

    6.13.6.13 subsidence;

    6.13.6.14 heave;

    6.13.6.15 landslip;

    6.13.6.16 collision;

    6.13.6.17 accidental damage to underground services;

    6.13.6.18 professional fees, demolition and site clearance costs; and

    6.13.6.19 public liability to anyone else.

6.13.7 Check part 2 to see if we require you to obtain before completion the insurer's confirmation that the insurer will notify us if the policy is not renewed or is cancelled or if you do not obtain this, report to us (see part 2).

6.13.8 Check part 2 to see if we require you to send us a copy of the buildings insurance policy and the last premium receipt to us.

7. OTHER OCCUPIERS

7.1 Rights or interests of persons who are not a party to the mortgage and who are or will be in occupation of the property may affect our rights under the mortgage, for example as overriding interests.

7.2 If your instructions state the name of a person who is to live at the property, you should ask the borrower before completing the mortgage that the information given by us in our mortgage instructions or mortgage offer about occupants is correct and nobody else is to live at the property.

7.3 Unless we state otherwise (see part 2), you must obtain a signed deed or form of consent from all occupants aged 17 or over of whom you are aware who are not a party to the mortgage before completion of the mortgage.

7.4 We recognise that in some cases the information given to us or you by a borrower may be incorrect or misleading. If you have any reason to doubt the accuracy of any information disclosed, you should report it to us (see part 2) provided the borrower agrees; if the borrower does not agree, you should return our instructions.

8. SEPARATE REPRESENTATION

Unless we otherwise state (see part 2), you must not advise:

8.1 any borrower who does not personally benefit from the loan; or

8.2 any guarantor; or

8.3 anyone intending to occupy the property who is to execute a consent to the mortgage, and you must arrange for them to see an independent conveyancer. If we do allow you to advise any of these people, you must only do so after recommending in the absence of any other person interested in the transaction that such person obtains independent legal advice. Any advice that you give any of these people must also be given in the absence of any other person interested in the transaction. You should be particularly careful if the matrimonial home is being charged to secure a business debt.

9. INDEMNITY INSURANCE

You must effect an indemnity insurance policy whenever the Lenders' Handbook identifies that this is an acceptable or required course to use to ensure that the property has a good and marketable title at completion. This paragraph does not relate to mortgage indemnity insurance. The draft policy should not be sent to us unless we ask for it. Check part 2 to see if the policy must be sent to us after completion. Where indemnity insurance is effected:

9.1 you must approve the terms of the policy on our behalf; and

9.2 the limit of indemnity must meet our requirements (see part 2); and

9.3 the policy must be effected without cost to us; and

9.4 you must disclose to the insurer all relevant information which you have obtained; and

9.5 the policy must not contain conditions which you know would make it void or prejudice our interests; and

9.6 you must provide a copy of the policy to the borrower and explain to the borrower why the policy was effected and that a further policy may be required if there is further lending against the security of the property; and

9.7 you must explain to the borrower that the borrower will need to comply with any conditions of the policy and that the borrower should notify us of any notice or potential claim in respect of the policy; and

9.8 the policy should always be for our benefit and, if possible, for the benefit of the borrower and any subsequent owner or mortgagee. If the borrower will not be covered by the policy, you must advise the borrower of this.

10. THE LOAN AND CERTIFICATE OF TITLE

10.1 You should not submit your certificate of title unless it is unqualified or we have authorised you in writing to proceed notwithstanding any issues you have raised with us.

10.2 We shall treat the submission by you of the certificate of title as a request for us to release the mortgage advance to you. Check part 2 to see if the mortgage advance will be paid electronically or by cheque and the minimum number of days notice we require. See part 2 for any standard deductions which may be made from the mortgage advance.

10.3 You are only authorised to release the loan when you hold sufficient funds to complete the purchase of the property and pay all stamp duties and registration fees to perfect the security as a first legal mortgage or, if you do not have them, you accept responsibility to pay them yourself. You must hold the loan on trust for us until completion. If completion is delayed, you must return it to us when and how we tell you (see part 2).

10.4 You should note that although your certificate of title will be addressed to us, we may at some time transfer our interest in the mortgage. In those circumstances, our successors in title to the mortgage and persons deriving title under or through the mortgage will also rely on your certificate.

10.5 If, after you have requested the mortgage advance, completion is delayed you must telephone or fax us immediately after you are aware of the delay and you must inform us of the new date for completion (see part 2).

10.6 See part 2 for details of how long you can hold the mortgage advance before returning it to us. If completion is delayed for longer than that period, you must return the mortgage advance to us. If you do not, we reserve the right to require you to pay interest on the amount of the mortgage advance (see part 2).

10.7 If the mortgage advance is not returned within the period set out in part 2, we will assume that the mortgage has been completed, and we will charge the borrower interest under the mortgage. We may make further payments and advances without reference to you.

11. THE DOCUMENTATION

11.1 The Mortgage

The mortgage incorporates our current mortgage conditions and, where applicable, loan conditions. If the mortgage conditions booklet is supplied to you with your instructions you must give it to the borrower before completion of the mortgage.

11.2 Explanation

You should explain to each borrower (and any other person signing or executing a document) his responsibilities and liabilities under the documents referred to in 11.1 and any documents he is required to sign.

11.3 Signing and Witnessing of Documents

It is considered good practice that the signature of a document that needs to be witnessed is witnessed by a solicitor, legal executive or licensed conveyancer. All documents required at completion must be dated with the date of completion of the loan.

12. INSTALMENT MORTGAGES AND MORTGAGE ADVANCES RELEASED IN INSTALMENTS

12.1 Introduction

12.1.1 If the cost of the building is to be paid by instalments as work progresses (for example, under a building contract) the amount of each instalment which we will be able to release will be based on a valuation made by our valuer at the time. Whilst we will not be bound by the terms of any building contract we will meet the reasonable requirements of the borrower and the builder as far as possible.

12.1.2 The borrower is expected to pay for as much work as possible from his own resources before applying to us for the first instalment. However, we may, if required, consider advancing a nominal sum on receipt of the certificate of title to enable the mortgage to be completed so long as the legal estate in the property is vested in the borrower.

12.1.3 The borrower is responsible for our valuer's fees for interim valuations as well as the first and final valuations.

12.2 Applications for Part of the Advance

As in the case of a normal mortgage account, cheques for instalment mortgages will be made payable and sent to you. However, instalment cheques (apart from the first which will be sent to you to enable you to complete the mortgage) can be made payable to and sent direct to the borrower on request.

12.3 Requests for Intermediate Cheques

To allow time for a valuation to be carried out, your request should be sent to us (see part 2) at least 10 days before the cheque is required.

12.4 Building Contract as Security

We will not lend on the security of a building contract unless our instructions to you specifically state to the contrary. As a result, the mortgage must not be completed and no part of the advance released until the title to the legal estate in the property has been vested in the borrower.

13. MORTGAGE INDEMNITY INSURANCE OR HIGH LOAN TO VALUE FEE

You are reminded to tell the borrower that we (and not the borrower) are the insured under any mortgage indemnity or similar form of insurance policy and that the insurer will have a subrogated right to claim against the borrower if it pays us under the policy. Different lenders call the various schemes of this type by different names. They may not involve an insurance policy.

REMINDERS: 6 CML LENDERS' HANDBOOK

14. AFTER COMPLETION

14.1 Application to HM Land Registry

14.1.1 You must register our mortgage at HM Land Registry. Before making your Land Registry application for registration, you must place a copy of the Land or Charge Certificate relating to the property on your file together with certified copies of the transfer, mortgage deed and any receipt or DS1 from a previous mortgagee.

14.1.2 Our mortgage conditions and mortgage deed have been deposited at HM Land Registry and it is therefore unnecessary to submit a copy of the mortgage conditions on an application for registration.

14.1.3 Where the loan is to be made in instalments or there is any deferred interest retention or stage release, check part 2 to see whether you must apply to the Land Registry on form 113 for entry of a notice on the register that we are under an obligation to make further advances. If the Land Registry code 'CHOBL' appears on the mortgage deed (it is usually in the top right hand corner) there is no need to submit a form 113.

14.1.4 The application for registration must be received by the Land Registry during the priority period afforded by your original Land Registry search made before Completion and, in any event, in the case of an application for first registration, within two months of completion.

14.2 Title Deeds

14.2.1 All title deeds, searches, enquiries, consents, requisitions and documents relating to the property in your possession must be held to our order and you must not create or exercise any lien over them. Unless otherwise instructed, they must be sent to us (see part 2) with the schedule supplied by us as soon as possible after completion. We expect them to be lodged, in any event, within three months of completion. If it is not possible to return the deeds to us within this period you should advise us in writing with a copy of any correspondence from HM Land Registry explaining the delay.

14.2.2 You must only send us documents we tell you to (see part 2). You should obtain the borrower's instructions concerning the retention of documents we tell you not to send us.

14.3 Your Mortgage File

14.3.1 For evidential purposes you must keep your file for at least six years from the date of the mortgage before destroying it. Microfiching or data imaging is suitable compliance with this requirement. It is the practice of some fraudsters to demand the conveyancing file on completion in order to destroy evidence that may later be used against them. It is important to retain these documents to protect our interests. Where you are processing personal data (as defined in the Data Protection Act 1998) on our behalf, you must;

14.3.1.1 take such security measures as are required to enable you to comply with obligations equivalent to those imposed on us by the seventh data protection principle in the 1998 Act; and

14.3.1.2 process such personal data only in accordance with our instructions. In addition, you must allow us to conduct such reasonable audit of your information security measures as we require to ensure your compliance with your obligations in this paragraph.

14.3.2 Subject to any right of lien or any overriding duty of confidentiality, you should treat documents comprising your file as if they are jointly owned by the borrower and the lender and you should not part with them without the consent of both parties. You should on request supply certified copies of documents on the file or a certified copy of the microfiche to either the borrower or the lender, and may make a reasonable charge for copying and certification.

15. LEGAL COSTS

Your charges and disbursements are payable by the borrower and should be collected from the borrower on or before completion. You must not allow non-payment of fees or disbursements to delay the stamping and registration of documents. The Law Society recommends that your costs for acting on our behalf in connection with the mortgage should, in the interest of transparency, be separately identified to the borrower.

16. TRANSACTIONS DURING THE LIFE OF THE MORTGAGE

16.1 Requests for Deeds

All requests for deeds should be made in writing and sent to us (see part 2). In making such a request you must have the consent of all of the borrowers to apply for the deeds.

16.2 Further Advances

16.2.1 Our mortgage secures further advances. Consequently, when a further advance is required for alterations or improvements to the property we will not normally instruct a member of our conveyancing panel.

16.2.2 If additional land is to be mortgaged or the further advance is required for some other purpose (for example, to purchase a spouse's equitable or other interest in the property), you may receive instructions to act for us in connection with that transaction.

16.3 Transfers of Equity

16.3.1 You must approve the transfer (which should be in the Land Registry's standard form) and, if we require, the deed of covenant on our behalf. Check part 2 to see if we have standard forms of transfer and deed of covenant. When drafting or approving a transfer, you should bear in mind:

16.3.1.1 although the transfer should state that it is subject to the mortgage (identified by date and parties), it need give no details of the terms of the mortgage;

16.3.1.2 the transfer need not state the amount of the mortgage debt. If it does, the figure should include both principal and interest at the date of completion, which you must check (see part 2 for where to obtain this);

16.3.1.3 there should be no statement that all interest has been paid to date.

16.3.2 You must ensure that every person who will be a borrower after the transfer covenants with us to pay the money secured by the mortgage, except in the case of:

16.3.2.1 an original party to the mortgage (unless the mortgage conditions are being varied); or

16.3.2.2 a person who has previously covenanted to that effect.

16.3.3 Any such covenant will either be in the transfer or in a separate deed of covenant. In a transfer, the wording of the covenant should be as follows, or as close as circumstances permit:

'The new borrower agrees to pay the lender all the money due under the mortgage and will keep to all the terms of the mortgage.'

If it is in the transfer, you must place a certified copy of the transfer with the deeds (unless we tell you not to in part 2).

16.3.4 If we have agreed to release a borrower or a guarantor and our standard transfer form (if any) includes no appropriate clause, you must add a simple form of release. The release clause should be as follows, or as close as circumstances permit:

'The lender releases ... from [his/her/their] obligations under the mortgage.'

You should check whether a guarantor who is to be released was a party to the mortgage or to a separate guarantee.

16.3.5 You must obtain the consent of every guarantor of which you are aware to the release of a borrower or, as the case may be, any other guarantor.

16.3.6 You must only submit the transfer to us for execution if it releases a party. All other parties must execute the transfer before it is sent to us. See part 2 for where the transfer should be sent for sealing. Part 2 also gives our approved form of attestation clause.

16.4 Properties To Be Let After Completion

16.4.1 You should advise the borrower that any letting of the property is prohibited without our prior consent. If the borrower wishes to let the property after completion then an application for consent should be made to us (see part 2). Check part 2 to see whether it is necessary to send to us a copy of the proposed tenancy when making the application.

16.4.2 If the application for our consent is approved and we instruct you to act for us, you must approve the form of tenancy agreement on our behalf.

16.4.3 Please also note that:

16.4.3.1 an administration fee will be payable for our consideration of the application whether or not consent is granted; and

16.4.3.2 the proposed rent should cover the borrower's gross mortgage payments at the time; and

16.4.3.3 we reserve the right to charge a higher rate of interest to the borrower in certain circumstances or change the terms of the mortgage.

16.5 Deeds of Variation, Rectification, Easement or Option Agreements

16.5.1 If we consent to any proposal for a deed of variation, rectification, easement or option agreement, we will rely on you to approve the documents on our behalf.

16.5.2 Our consent will usually be forthcoming provided that you first of all confirm in writing to us (see part 2) that our security will not be adversely affected in any way by entering into the deed. If you are able to provide this confirmation then we will not normally need to see a draft of the deed. If you cannot provide confirmation and we need to consider the matter in detail then an additional administration fee is likely to be charged.

16.5.3 Whether we are a party to the deed or give a separate deed or form of consent is a matter for your discretion. It should be sent to us (see part 2) for sealing or signing with a brief explanation of the reason for the document and its effect together with your confirmation that it will not adversely affect our security.

16.6 Deeds of Postponement or Substitution

If we agree to enter into an arrangement with other lenders concerning the order of priority of their mortgages, you will be supplied with our standard form of deed or form of postponement or substitution. We will normally not agree to any amendments to the form. In no cases will we postpone our first charge over the property.

17. REDEMPTION

17.1 Redemption Statement

17.1.1 When requesting a redemption statement you should quote the expected repayment date and whether you are acting for the borrower or have the borrower's authority to request the redemption statement in addition to the information mentioned in paragraph 2.1. You should request this at least five working days before the expected redemption date. You must quote all the borrower's mortgage account or roll numbers of which you are aware when requesting the repayment figure. You must only request a redemption statement if you are acting for the borrower or have the borrower's written authority to request a redemption statement.

17.1.2 To guard against fraud please ensure that if payment is made by cheque then the redemption cheque is made payable to us and you quote the mortgage account or roll number and name of borrower.

17.2 Discharge

On the day of completion you should send the discharge and your remittance for the repayment to us (see part 2). Check part 2 to see if we discharge via a DS1 form or direct with the Land Registry.

Part 2 is not reproduced in this booklet.

Checklists

7.1 Lease checklist

(1) Check the lease term. Is it sufficient for the client? Does it comply with the CML Lenders' Handbook?

(2) Does a management company exist? Carry out a company search.

(3) What are the forfeiture provisions? Most lenders will not accept a bankruptcy provision.

(4) Are the insurance provisions adequate? What will happen in the event of frustration?

(5) Check that the lease is complete and correctly executed.

(6) What are the arrangements for the service charge? Is the proportion collected correct? Obtain and check accounts for the last three years. Obtain written confirmation that no large expenditure is anticipated which would lead to an increase in the current payments. Is the service charge paid in stages?

(7) Check carefully if consent is required to assign the lease. If so, what are the landlord's requirements? Are they fair? Find out what they are prior to exchange of contracts and ensure that your clients can fulfil them. Who will pay the costs of obtaining the consent?

(8) Does the lessee hold a share in the management company? Make sure you obtain a signed stock transfer form and arrange for your clients to sign a blank form by completion to place with the deeds.

(9) Has the lease been varied? If so, has the deed of variation been registered? Are any further variations necessary? Are the enforcing covenants sufficient?

(10) Check each clause carefully. If you are unsure on any matters, seek advice!

(11) What is the position concerning payment of rent? Is there a rent review clause which will come into operation in the future? Work out what the new rent would be and check carefully what the new rent will represent. Some leases provide that the new rent willl be a percentage of the market value of the property at the rent review date. Others provide that it will be a percentage of the value of the entire building.

(12) What rights exist in favour of the property. Are they sufficient? Can the lessee freely pass over the entire development and use the gardens and parking areas?

(13) What reservations are there? Can the freeholder develop the building further? Make sure your client is aware of the freeholder's rights.

(14) Find out how much the fee for notice of assignment is, and make a note on the file to serve notice as soon as completion has taken place.

(15) What is the position for future alterations? Ask the client if he intends to alter the property.

(16) Make sure the client receives a copy of the lease and service charge accounts.

REMINDERS: 7 CHECKLISTS

(17) Obtain an up-to-date insurance schedule and copy of the policy. Is the cover sufficient for the lender's needs?

(18) Provide a report to the client on the lease, and explain any options for extending the lease and purchasing the freehold.

7.2 Purchase of a new property - checklist

There follow some key points to consider when acting in the purchase of a new property. Of course, careful consideration must be given to the specific requirements of each particular transaction.

Exchange of contracts

(1) It is very likely that the developer/seller will impose a deadline for exchange of contracts (usually about 14 days!). Consider whether this is realistic, especially if your client is involved in a chain. If necessary, advise your client and all parties that more time may be required.

Completion on notice

(2) If a fixed completion date cannot be agreed and completion will be on notice, ensure that a sufficient notice period is provided for in the contract to allow for re-inspection by the client and his surveyor. It is likely that the same notice period will need to be agreed on any related sale.

'Long stop' completion date

(3) Try to agree a long stop completion date even if this is quite distant. Remember that any mortgage offer and its terms will only be valid for a limited period. Ask the developer for a note of the anticipated structure completion date.

Exchange of contracts subject to searches, etc

(4) If you are instructed by your client to exchange contracts subject to a local search and mortgage offer, ensure that the conditions strike an equal balance for both parties. If your client has asked his lender for a particular fixed or discounted interest rate, then it is important that the clause dealing with the mortgage offer reflects the need for the offer to be satisfactory to the buyer in all respects. Make sure that any condition dealing with a search covers 'all' searches to be made, not just the local search. For example, it should cover any environmental search to be made.

Services

(5) Ask your client to check which services will be connected on completion or whether he needs to organise this.

REMINDERS: 7 CHECKLISTS

Land and drainage

(6) Does the contract deal with any road and drainage agreements to be entered into with supporting bonds? If these are not available, you may need to agree a retention to comply with the CML Lenders' Handbook and should seek advice from the mortgage valuer as to the correct amount to be retained.

NHBC

(7) Check whether an NHBC guarantee will be needed, and ensure that the developer is registered.

Re-inspection

(8) Remind the client of the need to re-inspect the property prior to completion.

Transfer plan

(9) Provide the client with a copy of any transfer plan as soon as possible so that he can check its accuracy.

Registration

(10) On exchange of contracts, consider whether you need to register the contract at the Land Registry to protect your client's interest.

# The Law Society's Code for Completion by Post

8.1 Law Society's Code for Completion by Post

Before agreeing to adopt this code, a solicitor/licenced conveyancer must be satisfied that doing so will not be contrary to the interests of the client (including any mortgagee client).

When adopted, the code applies without variation, unless agreed to in writing in advance.

Procedure

General

1. To adopt this code, all the solicitors must expressly agree, preferably in writing, to use it to complete a specific transaction.

2. On completion, the seller's solicitor acts as the buyer's solicitor's agent without any fee or disbursements.

Before completion

3. The seller's solicitor will specify in writing to the buyer's solicitor before completion the mortgages or charges secured on the property which, on or before completion, will be redeemed or discharged to the extent that they relate to the property.

4. The seller's solicitor *undertakes*:

    (i) to have the seller's authority to receive the purchase money on completion;

    and

    (ii) on completion to have the authority of the proprietor of each mortgage to charge specified under paragraph 3 to receive the sum intended to repay it,

    BUT

    if the seller's solicitor does not have all the necessary authorities then:

    (iii) to advise the buyer's solicitor no later than 4 p.m. on the working day before the completion date that they do not have all the authorities or immediately if any is withdrawn later, and

    (iv) not to complete until he or she has the buyer's solicitor's instructions.

REMINDERS: 8 LAW SOCIETY'S CODE FOR COMPLETION BY POST

5. Before the completion date, the buyer's solicitor will send the seller's solicitor instructions as to any of the following which apply:

   (i) documents to be examined and marked;

   (ii) memoranda to be endorsed;

   (iii) undertakings to be given;

   (iv) deeds, documents (including any relevant undertakings) and authorities relating to rents, deposits, keys etc. to be send to the buyer's solicitor following completion; and

   (v) other relevant matters.

   In default of instructions, the seller's solicitor is under no duty to examine, mark or endorse any document.

6. The buyer's solicitor will remit to the seller's solicitor the sum required to complete, as notified in writing on the seller's solicitor's completion statement or otherwise, or in default of notification as shown by the contract. If the funds are remitted by transfer between banks, the seller's solicitor will instruct the receiving bank to telephone to report immediately the funds have been received. Pending completion, the seller's solicitor will hold the funds to the buyer's solicitor's order.

7. If by the agreed date and time for completion the seller's solicitor has not received the authorities specified in paragraph 4, instructions under paragraph 5 and the sum specified in paragraph 6, the seller's solicitor will forthwith notify the buyer's solicitor and require further instructions.

   Completion

8. The seller's solicitor will complete forthwith on receiving the sum specified in paragraph 6, or at a later time agreed with the buyer's solicitor.

9. When completing, the seller's solicitor *undertakes*:

   (i) to comply with the instructions given under paragraph 5; and

   (ii) to redeem or obtain discharges for every mortgage or charge so far as it relates to the property specified under paragraph 3 which has not already been redeemed or discharged.

   After completion

10. The seller's solicitor *undertakes*:

    (i) immediately completion has taken place to hold to the buyer's solicitor's order every item referred to in (iv) of paragraph 5 and not to exercise a lien over any such item;

REMINDERS: 8 LAW SOCIETY'S CODE FOR COMPLETION BY POST

 (ii) as soon as possible after completion, and in any event on the same day,

  (a) to confirm to the buyer's solicitor by telephone or fax that completion has taken place;

 and

  (b) to send written confirmation and, at the risk of the buyer's solicitor, the items listed in (iv) of paragraph 5 to the buyer's solicitor by first class post or document exchange.

Supplementary

11. The rights and obligations of the parties, under the contract or otherwise, are not affected by this code.

12.

 (i) Reference to the seller's solicitor and the buyer's solicitor apply as appropriate to solicitors acting for other parties who adopt the code.

 (ii) When a licensed conveyancer adopts this code, references to a solicitor include a licensed conveyancer.

13. A dispute or difference arising between solicitors who adopt this code (whether or not subject to any variation) relating directly to its application is to be referred to a single arbitrator within one month. If they do not agree on the appointment within one month, the President or the Law Society may appoint the arbitrator at the request of one of the solicitors.

Law Society Guidance

9.1 'Pink Card' – Warning on Undertakings

Remember that there is NO obligation on a solicitor to give an undertaking, even to assist the progress of a client's matter.

Be SMART when giving undertakings – make sure they are:

S Specific

Undertakings should refer to a particular task or action which has been clearly identified and defined. Do not give general or open-ended undertakings, such as an undertaking to discharge 'all outstanding mortgages on a property' or 'the usual undertaking'. Make sure that any undertaking to pay monies out of a fund is qulified by the proviso that the fund comes into your hands, **and** that it is sufficient.

M Measurable

Undertakings should contain agreed measures or steps which are understood by both parties and can easily be monitored or checked, so that there can be no dispute as to whether an undertaking has been fully discharged. If an undertaking involves the payment of a sum of money, make sure the amount is clear or that it is easy to calculate. Ambiguous undertakings will be construed in favour of the recipient.

A Agreed

Undertakings should be expressly agreed by both the person giving and the person receiving them and should be confirmed in writing. They may be given orally or in writing and need not necessarily include the word 'undertake' – beware of inadvertant undertakings.

R Realistic

Undertakings should be achievable. Before giving an undertaking consider carefully whether you will be able to implement it. If any events must happen before you will be able to implement your undertaking, it is good practice to spell out those events on the face of your undertaking. An undertaking is still binding even if it is to do something outside your control. As you give the undertaking – you can stay in control.

T Timed

Undertakings should indicate when, or on the happening of which event, they will be implemented. In the absence of an express term, there is an implied term that an undertaking will be performed within a reasonable time, having regard to its nature.

REMINDERS: 9 LAW SOCIETY GUIDANCE

General points

Costs

- Don't ask other solicitors to provide an undertaking in terms you would not give yourself. This applies particularly to undertakings as to costs: it's unfair to expect another solicitor to give an open-ended undertaking to pay your costs. Be prepared to give an upper limit or agree a basis of charging.
- An undertaking to pay another party's costs is generally discharged if the matter does not proceed to completion. If you intend some other arrangement, make this clear.

Conveyancing

- The Law Society's formulae for exchange of contracts and its code for completion by post contain certain undertakings. Are you sure that you and your staff really know what undertakings they are giving in a normal conveyancing transaction?
- Make sure that each of your replies to requistions on title concerning mortgages specifies exactly which mortgages or charges you intend to discharge. Vague replies will probably result in you being liable to discharge all charges, whether you know them or not!
- Do not give unconditional undertakings without sufficient enquiry into the amount owed on prior charges – don't always rely on what your client tells you. Where necessary, obtain a provisional redemption figure.
- If your ability to comply with an undertaking depends on action to be taken by another solicitor, make sure that he or she will be able to comply, eg by obtaining an undertaking to a similar effect.
- Beware of bank 'standard form' undertakings – they sometimes go beyond what is in your control – it may be necessary to amend them.

Good Management

- Principals are responsible for undertakings given by staff. Clear guidance should be given to staff, specifying those premitted to give undertakings and prescribing the manner in which they can be given. Find how safe you are by doing an 'undertaking audit' – ask staff to check files for undischarged undertakings. Note how many have been given in a sloppy or negligent manner and calculate the size of the potential claims if things go wrong. Then introduce a system to put things right. This might be to:

    - draw up standard undertakings for use, where possible, by all fee earners, with any deviation from the norm to be authorised by a partner;
    - have all undertakings checked by another fee earner prior to being given (or at least those which amount to financial obligation);
    - make a note on the file and/or in a central register that an undertaking has been given and ensure that it has been properly discharged before closing the file.

REMINDERS: 9 LAW SOCIETY GUIDANCE

9.2 Contaminated Land – the Warning Card

Warning – To All Solicitors – Contaminated Land Liabilities

The advice contained on this Card is not intended to be a professional requirement for solicitors. Solicitors should be aware of the requirements of Part IIA of the Environmental Protection Act 1990 but they themselves cannot provide their clients with conclusive answers. They must exercise their professional judgement to determine the applicability of this advice to each matter and, where necessary, they should suggest to the client obtaining specialist advice. In the view of the Law Society the advice contained in this Card conforms to current best practice.

Solicitors should be aware that the environmental liabilities may arise and consider what further enquiries and specialist assistance the client should be advised to obtain.

Contaminated Land

(1) The contaminated land regime was brought into effect in England on 1 April 2000. It applied to all land, whether residential, commercial, industrial or agricultural. It can affect owners, occupiers, developers, and lenders. The legislation, which is contained in Part IIA of the Environmental Protection Act 1990 and in regulations and statutory guidance issued under it (see Contaminated Land (England) Regulations 2000, SI 2000/227 and DETR Guidance on Contaminated Land April 2000) is retrospective. It covers existing and future contamination.

The National Assembly is expected shortly to introduce similar regulations regarding contaminated land in Wales.

(2) Local authorities must inspect and identify seriously contaminated sites. They can issue remediation notices requiring action to remediate contamination, in the absence of a voluntary agreement to do so. In certain cases ('Special Sites') responsibility for enforcement lies with the Environment Agency.

A negative reply to the standard local authority enquiries from the local authority may merely mean that the site has not been inspected. It does not necessarily mean that there is no problem.

Compliance can be costly, and may result in expenditure which could exceed the value of the property.

Liability falls primarily on those who 'cause or knowingly permit' contamination (a Class A person). If the authority cannot identify a Class A person, liability falls on a Class B person, the current owner, or occupier of the land. Class B persons include lenders in possession. There are complex exclusion provisions for transferring liability from one party to another. Some exclusions apply only on the transfer of land, or the grant of a lease. The applicability of any relevant exclusion needs to be considered before entering such transactions.

In every transaction you must consider whether contamination is an issue.

Conveyancing Transactions

In purchases, mortgages and leases, solicitors should:

REMINDERS: 9 LAW SOCIETY GUIDANCE

(1) Advise the client of potential liabilities associated with contaminated land.

Generally clients should be advised of the possibility and consequences of acquiring interests in contaminated land and the steps that can be taken to assess the risks.

(2) Make specific enquiries of the seller.

In all commercial cases, and if contamination is considered likely to be a risk in residential cases (eg redevelopment of brown field land):

(3) Make enquiries of statutory and regulatory bodies.

(4) Undertake independent site history investigation, eg obtaining site report from commercial company.

In commercial cases, if there is a likelihood that the site is contaminated:

(5) Advise independent full site investigation.

(6) Consider use of contractual provisions and exclusion tests.

This may involve specific disclosure of known defects, possibly coupled with price reduction, requirements on seller to remedy before completion, and in complex cases the use of warranties and indemnities.

For unresolved problems, consider:

(7) Advising withdrawal, and noting advice.

(8) Advising insurance (increasingly obtainable for costs of remediation of undetected contamination and any shortfall in value because of undisclosed problems).

Specific Transactions

(1) Leases

Consider if usual repair and statutory compliance clauses transfer remediation liability to client and advise.

(2) Mortgages

Advise lender, if enquiries reveal potential for or existence of contamination, and seek instructions. In enforcement cases, consider appointment of receivers, rather than steps resulting in lender becoming mortgagee in possession, and so treated as a Class B person.

(3) Share sales and asset purchases.

Consider recommending the obtaining of specialist technical advice on potential liabilities, use of detailed enquiries, warranties and indemnities.

Other Relevant Legislation

Other legislation and common law liabilities (eg nuisance) may also be relevant when advising on environmental matters, including:

- Water Resources Act 1991
- Groundwater Regulations 1998
- Pollution Prevention and Control (England and Wales) Regulations 2000.

9.3 'Green Card' Warning on Property Fraud

Could you spot a property fraud?

The signs to watch for include the following (but this list is not exhaustive):

- **Fraudulent buyer or fictitious solicitors** – especially if the buyer is introduced to your practice by a third party (for example a broker or estate agent) who is not well known to you. Beware of clients whom you never meet and solicitors not known to you.
- **Unusual instructions** – for example a solicitor being instructed by the seller to remit the net proceeds of sale to anyone other than the seller.
- **Misrepresentation of the purchase price** – ensure that the true cash price actually to be paid is stated as the consideration in the contract and transfer and is identical to the price shown in the mortgage instructions and in the report on title to the lender.
- **A deposit or any part of purchase price paid direct** – a deposit or the difference between the mortgage advance and the price, paid direct, or said to be paid direct, to the seller.
- **Incomplete contract documentation** – contract documents not fully completed by the seller's representative, ie dates missing or the identity of the parties not fully described or financial details not fully stated.
- **Changes in the purchase price** – adjustments to the purchase price, particularly in high percentage mortgage cases, or allowances off the purchase price, for example, for works to be carried out.
- **Unusual transactions** – transactions which do not follow their normal course or the usual pattern of events:

    (a) client with current mortgage on two or more properties

    (b) client using an alias

    (c) client buying several properties from same person or two or more persons using same solicitor

    (d) client reselling property at a substantial profit, for which no explanation has been provided.

What steps can I take to minimise the risk of fraud?

Be vigilant: if you have any doubts about a transaction, consider whether any of the following steps could be taken to minimise the risk of fraud:

- **Verify the identity and *bone fides* of your client and solicitors' firms you do not know** – meet the clients where possible and get to know them a little. Check that the solicitor's firm and office address appear in the *Directory of Solicitors and Barristers* or contact the Law Society's Regulation and Information Services (tel: 0870 606 2555).
- **Question unusual instructions** – if you receive unusual instructions from your client discuss them with your client fully.
- **Discuss with your client any aspects of the transaction which worry you** – if, for example, you have any suspicion that your client may have submitted a false

REMINDERS: 9 LAW SOCIETY GUIDANCE

mortgage application or references, or if the lender's valuation exceeds the actual price paid, discuss this with your client. If you believe that the client intends to proceed with a fraudulent application, you must refuse to continue to act for the buyer and lender.

- **Check that the true price is shown on all documents** – check that the actual price paid is stated in the contract, transfer and mortgage instructions. Where you are also acting for a lender, tell your client that you will have to cease acting unless the client permits you to report to the lender all allowances and incentives. See also the guidance price in [1990] *Gazette*, 12 December, 16 (see Annex 25F, p 500 in the Guide).

- **Do not witness pre-signed documentation** – no document should be witnessed by a solicitor or his or her staff unless the person signing does so in the presence of the witness. If the document is pre-signed, ensure that it is re-signed in the presence of a witness.

- **Verify signatures** – consider whether signatures on all documents connected with a transaction should be examined and compared with signatures on any other available documentation.

- **Make a company search** – where a private company is the seller, or the seller has purchased from a private company in the recent past, and you suspect that the sale may not be on properly arm's length terms, you should make a search in the Companies Register to ascertain the names and addresses of the officers and shareholders, which can then be compared with the names of those connected with the transaction and the seller and buyer.

Remember that, even where investigations result in a solicitor ceasing to act for a client, the solicitor will owe a duty of confidentiality, which would prevent the solicitor passing on information to the lender. It is only where the solicitor is satisfied that there is a strong *prima facie* case that the client was using the solicitor to further a fraud or other criminal purposes that the duty of confidentiality would not apply.

Any failure to observe these signs and to take the appropriate steps may be used in court as evidence against you if you and your client are prosecuted, or if you are sued for negligence.

REMINDERS: 9 LAW SOCIETY GUIDANCE

9.4 'Blue Card' Money Laundering

Warning to all Solicitors

Could you be involved?

Could you or your firm be unwittingly assisting in the laundering of the proceeds of crime? The Criminal Justice Act 1993 and the Money Laundering Regulations 1993 mark an important step in the fight against serious crime, in particular against the drugs trade. All solicitors should be aware of the money laundering provisions in the Criminal Justice Act 1993. **Additionally**, solicitors who engage in investment business within the meaning of the Financial Services Act 1986 are subject to the Money Laundering Regulations 1993, and must take the steps required by the Regulations to ensure that they and their firms cannot be used by money launderers.

Might YOU commit a criminal offence?

The Criminal Justice Act 1993 is enforced in parts and the Money Laundering Regulations 1993 come into effect on **1st April 1994**. If solicitors do not take steps to learn about the provisions of the 1993 Act, they may commit criminal offences, by assisting someone known or suspected to be laundering money generated by any serious crime, by telling clients or anyone else that they are under investigation for an offence of money laundering, or by failing to report a suspicion of money laundering in the case of drug trafficking or terrorism, unless certain exceptions apply. **Additionally**, solicitors who engage in investment business within the meaning of the Financial Services Act 1986 will commit criminal offences unless they take the steps required by the Regulations.

As well as the Criminal Justice Act 1993 and the Money Laundering Regulations 1993, the law relating to money laundering in England and Wales is contained in several different Acts:

- The Drug Trafficking Offences Act 1986
- The Criminal Justice Act 1988
- The Prevention of Terrorism (Temporary Provisions) Act 1989
- The Criminal Justice (International Co-Operation) Act 1990.

The 1993 Act also amends parts of these Acts.

Guidance on the earlier Acts and their effects on solicitors can be found in Chapter 16 of the Guide to the Professional Conduct of Solicitors, 6th Edition. **Remember** – The Criminal Justice Act 1993 in some cases changes the client's right to confidentiality from his/her solicitor.

Could you spot a money laundering transaction?

The signs to watch for:

- **Unusual settlement requests** – settlement by cash of any large transaction involving the purchase or property or other investment should give rise to caution. Payment by way of third-party cheque or money transfer where there is a variation between

REMINDERS: 9 LAW SOCIETY GUIDANCE

the account holder, the signatory and a prospective investor should give rise to the need for additional enquiries.

- **Unusual instructions** – care should always be taken when dealing with a client who has no discernible reason for using the firm's service, eg clients with distant addresses who could find the same service nearer their home-base; or clients whose requirements do not fit into the normal pattern of the firm's business and could be more easily serviced elsewhere.
- **Large sums of cash** – always be cautious when requested to hold large sums of cash in your client account, either pending further instructions from the client or for no other purpose than for onward transmission to a third party.
- **The secretive client** – a personal client who is reluctant to provide details of his identity. Be particularly cautious about the client that you do not meet in person.
- **Suspect territories** – caution should be exercised whenever a client is introduced by an overseas bank, other investor or third party based in countries where production of drugs or drug trafficking may be prevalent.

Investment Business?

What the law says you must do

Solicitors who engage in investment business within the meaning of the Financial Services Act 1986 must comply with the provisions of the Money Laundering Regulations 1993. Every firm should keep a copy of the Regulations. In particular, every firm affected by the Regulations must:

(1) Ensure that all staff who handle investment business are given training in the recognition and handling of suspicious transactions. Every firm must ensure that employees are aware of the firm's policies and procedures for preventing money laundering.

(2) Appoint an individual to whom staff can report suspicions of money laundering, and who will be responsible for making a decision on reporting the suspicions outside the firm to the appropriate authorities.

(3) Ensure that they have in place a recognised procedure for obtaining satisfactory evidence of the identity of those with whom they do business, and that records of that evidence of identity are established and kept in respect of each transaction for five years. There are exceptions set out in Regulation 10.

(4) Establish and maintain for at least five years from the completion of the transactions, a record of each transaction undertaken.

(5) Report knowledge or suspicions to the Financial Unit, National Criminal Intelligence Service, PO Box 8000, London SE11 5EN. Telephone 020 7238 8282.

REMINDERS: 9 LAW SOCIETY GUIDANCE

Further advice and guidance can be obtained from the Law Society:

The Law Society's Professional Adviser in the Court Business Team of the Legal Practice Directorate, The Law Society, 113 Chancery Lane, London WC2A 1PL, Tel: 020 7242 1222, Fax: 020 7831 0344.

The Joint Money Laundering Steering Group Information Transfer Ltd
Burleigh House
15 Newmarket Road
Cambridge CB5 8EG
Tel: 01223 312227
Fax: 01223 310200

Addresses

10.1 Land Registry Offices and Telephone Numbers

HM Land Registry Headquarters

Lincoln's Inn Fields
London
WC2A 3PH
DX No: 1098 London/Chancery Lane WC2
Tel: 020 7917 8888
Fax: 020 7955 0110
www.landreg.gov.uk

Land Charges Department

Drakes Hill Court
Burrington Way
Plymouth
PL5 3LP
DX No: 8249 Plymouth (3)
Tel: 01752 635600
Fax: 01752 766666
www.lrdirect.co.uk

Land Registry Telephone Services

These numbers deal with all telephone services including land charges services. Telephone services for Wales specialise in Welsh names and offer a Welsh-speaking service.

All calls are charged at local rates.

Telephone services: 0845 308 4545
Telephone services for Wales: 0845 307 4535

ADDRESSES

Birkenhead (Old Market)
Tel: 0151 473 1110
DX: 14300 Birkenhead (3)

Birkenhead (Rosebrae)
Tel: 0151 472 6666
DX: 24270 Birkenhead (4)

Coventry
Tel: 024 7686 0860
DX: 18900 Coventry (3)

Croydon
Tel: 020 8781 9103
DX: 2699 Croydon (3)

District Land Registry for Lancashire
Tel: 01772 836700
DX: 721560 Lytham St Annes (6)

Durham (Boldon House)
Tel: 0191 301 2345
DX: 60860 Durham (6)

Durham (Southfield House)
Tel: 0191 301 3500
DX: 60200 Durham (3)

Gloucester
Tel: 01452 511111
DX: 7599 Gloucester (3)

Harrow
Tel: 020 8235 1181
DX: 4299 Harrow (4)

HM Land Registry Headquarters
Tel: 020 7917 8888
DX: 1098 London/Chancery Lane

Kingston Upon Hull
Tel: 01482 223244
DX: 26700 Hull (4)

Land Charges Department
Tel: 01752 636666
DX: 8249 Plymouth (3)

Leicester
Tel: 0116 265 4000
DX: 11900 Leicester (5)

Lytham
Tel: 01253 849849
DX: 14500 Lytham St Annes (3)

Nottingham (East)
Tel: 0115 906 5353
DX: 10298 Nottingham (3)

Peterborough
Tel: 01733 288288
DX: 12598 Peterborough (4)

Plymouth
Tel: 01752 636000
DX: 8299 Plymouth (4)

Portsmouth
Tel: 023 9276 8888
DX: 83550 Portsmouth (2)

Stevenage
Tel: 01438 788889
DX: 6099 Stevenage (2)

Swansea
Tel: 01792 458877
DX: 33700 Swansea (2)

Telford
Tel: 01952 290355
DX: 28100 Telford (2)

The District Land Registry for Wales
Tel: 01792 355000
DX: 82800 Swansea (2)

Tunbridge Wells
Tel: 01892 510015
DX: 3999 Tunbridge Wells (2)

Weymouth
Tel: 01305 363636
DX: 8799 Weymouth (2)

York
Tel: 01904 450000
DX: 61599 York (2)

10 addresses

ADDRESSES

10.2 Other useful addresses

Coal Authority
Mining Reports Department
200 Litchfield Lane
Berry Hill
Mansfield
Nottingham
NG18 4RG
Tel: 01623 427162
Fax: 01623 622072
DX: 716176 Mansfield (5)
www.coal.gov.uk

Companies House
Companies House
Crown Way
Cardiff
CF4 3UZ
Tel: 029 2038 8588
Fax: 029 2038 0900
DX: 33050 Cardiff (1)
www.companies-house.gov.uk

Council of Mortgage Lenders
3 Savile Row
London
W1X 1AF
Tel: 020 7437 0655
Fax: 020 7734 6416
DX: 81550 Savile Row W1
www.cml.org.uk

Court of Protection
Public Trust Office
Protection Division
Stewart House
24 Kingsway
London
WC2B 6JX
Tel: 020 7664 7000
Fax: 020 7664 7702
DX: 37965 Kingsway
www.publictrust.gov.uk

Environment Agency (Head Office)
Rio House
Waterside Drive
Aztec West
Almondsbury
Bristol
BS32 4UD
Tel: 01454 624400
Fax: 01454 624409
DX: 121225 Almondsbury (2)
www.environment-agency.gov.uk

Institute of Legal Executives
Kempston Manor
Kempston
MK42 7AB
Tel: 01234 841000
Fax: 01234 840373
DX: 124780 Kempston (1)
www.ilex.org.uk

Law Society of England and Wales
The Law Society's Hall
113 Chancery Lane
London
WC2A 1PL
Tel: 020 7242 1222
Fax: 020 7831 0344
DX: 56 Lond/Chancery Lane WC2
www.lawsoc.org.uk

Leasehold Valuation Tribunal
Whittington House
19-30 Alfred Place
London
WC1E 7LR
Tel: 020 7446 7738
Fax: 020 7637 1250
www.housing.odpm.gov.uk/order/alvt/index.htm

ADDRESSES

National Association of Estate Agents
Arbon House
21 Jury Street
Warwick
Warwickshire
CV34 4EH
Tel: 01926 496800
Fax: 01926 400953
DX: 18120 Warwick
www.naea.co.uk

Office for the Supervision of Solicitors
Victoria Court
8 Dormer Place
Leamington Spa
Warwickshire
CV32 5AE
Tel: 01926 820082
Fax: 01926 431435
DX: 292320 Leamington Spa (4)
www.solicitors-online.com

Railtrack Property (Headquarters)
Railtrack House
Euston Square
London
NW1 2EE
Tel: 020 7557 8020
Fax: 020 7557 9121
www.discover-railtrack.co.uk

Royal Institution of Chartered Surveyors
12 Great George Street
Parliament Square
London
SW1P 3AD
Tel: 020 7222 7000
Fax: 020 7222 9430
DX: 2348 Victoria SW1
www.rics.org.uk